WITHDRAWN

JOHN F. KENNEDY AND THE
NEW PACIFIC COMMUNITY, 1961–63

Also by Timothy P. Maga

DEFENDING PARADISE: The United States and Guam, 1898–1950
AMERICA, FRANCE AND THE REFUGEE PROBLEM, 1933–47

John F. Kennedy and the New Pacific Community, 1961–63

Timothy P. Maga
Chair of History Program
University of Maryland Asian Division

St. Martin's Press   New York

First published in the United States of America in 1990

Phototypeset by Input Typesetting Ltd, London

Printed in Great Britain

ISBN 0–312–03639–6

Library of Congress Cataloging-in-Publication Data
Maga, Timothy P., *1952–*
John F. Kennedy and the New Pacific Community, 1961–3/Timothy P. Maga
p. cm
Includes bibliographical references.
ISBN 0–312–03639–6
1. United States—Foreign relations—1961–1963. 2. Kennedy, John F. (John
Fitzgerald), 1917–1963. 3. United States—Foreign relations—Pacific Area. 4.
Pacific Area—Foreign relations—United States. I. Title.
E841.M24 1990
973.922'092—dc20

To Diana and the family

Contents

Preface

Over a quarter century has passed since that snowy January day when John F. Kennedy told the world in his inaugural address: "We shall pay any price, bear any burden, meet any hardship, support any friend, oppose any foe to assure the survival and success of liberty." In 1961, those words sounded heroic. In the early 1990s, they have a far more ironic and ambiguous ring. Few Americans listening to that speech a generation later could avoid hearing, along with its pride and dedication, a tone of great arrogance – born out of idealism, perhaps, but pugnacious and sadly divorced from the intricacies of world politics. The years since the Kennedy inaugural have taught Americans a good deal about the limits of American power. The most painful lesson, of course, was the failure in Vietnam; a political and military débâcle in which many of the crucial early steps were taken by Kennedy himself.

Anxious to explain the mechanics and significance of this failure, authors ranging from David Halberstam, *The Best and the Brightest* (1972), to William Rust, *Kennedy in Vietnam* (1985), have treated Vietnam as an isolated incident within the Kennedy record. Boldly, they suggest that Vietnam symbolized Kennedy's Asian/Pacific policy, and then proceed without further allusion to that policy. Painting a bleak picture of what Secretary of State Dean Rusk politely called "the extremely frustrating task" of Washington's diplomacy in Vietnam, American journalists and historians have reconstructed the Kennedy administration's mounting concern over the communists' "liberation war" in Vietnam. They have also noted Kennedy's growing doubts over the reliability and effectiveness of South Vietnam's president Ngo Dinh Diem, and his somewhat reluctant but "inevitable" reliance on United States military involvements.

The military solution, according to the chroniclers, remained Kennedy's best way to compensate for Diem's weakness. Indeed, the Kennedy administration reasoned that there was no alternative other than military withdrawal. To Kennedy, a Vietnam withdrawal would constitute a denial of the "pay any price" inaugural promise to the international community. It might also stimulate unwanted political discussions at home. Washington's "frustrations" with this Vietnam dilemma led to the American-abetted plot in which Diem lost his

ix

life and United States commitments to the South Vietnamese government deepened. These accounts concerning the Kennedy phase of
the Vietnam tale usually end with comments on Kennedy's role in
the Diem murder, the former's own assassination, and the debate
over Kennedy's Vietnam options had he lived.

Despite the academic reliability of the "Kennedy and Vietnam"
works, there remains a certain incompleteness to the story. The
larger vision of Kennedy's New Frontier for the Asian/Pacific region
continues to be ignored. Kennedy and his cabinet spent a considerable amount of time designing a policy that would forever influence
events in specific and key areas within the Asian/Pacific theatre. In
spite of the drama of the Vietnam issues, much of it played out after
22 November 1963, the Kennedy administration also attached great
strategic, political, and economic significance to American relations
with Indonesia, Australia, Micronesia, the Philippines, Japan, and
the Ryukyus. Time and tragedy has clouded this reality; a reality
that embraced an "America can succeed at anything" philosophy.
With the exception of Indochina, the Asian/Pacific locations noted
above were seen by the Kennedy administration as peaceful symbols
of the developing Third World. They encompassed what the State
Department called "the New Pacific Community." Kennedy's effort
to translate New Frontier idealism into practical policy for the benefit
of peaceful "New Pacific Community" development and security
became a primary goal and component of his Asian/Pacific
diplomacy.

My book hopes to shed light on this forgotten policy and the place
of the "New Pacific Community" within it. Kennedy's endeavors to
influence events in the territories of the American Pacific, in the
nations of Australia, Indonesia, Japan and the Philippines, as well
as in the occupied Ryukyu islands, remain important aspects of
this work. As the Indochina problem worsened, Kennedy hoped to
balance his difficulties there with great success in other key areas of
the developing Asian/Pacific region. The region remained mysterious
to him. Yet, as a Pacific War veteran, he took a personal interest in
some Pacific matters and, according to most accounts, he sincerely
believed that American policy had neglected the best interests of
Pacific peoples for far too long. This personal conclusion was wedded
to the New Frontier mission of total commitment to the anti-communist crusade. That mission also included alleged humanist concerns,
innovative development policies, and national self-interest. To Kennedy, some combination of this difficult mission's components prom-

ised: (1) American-stimulated success in keeping the peace, (2) the development of the Asian/Pacific economies, and (3) the winning of the allegiance of Pacific peoples to the American-led anti-communist struggle.

When Kennedy's plans for Pacific peace and development met opposition from the New Pacific Community, his reaction remained in the realm of shocked disbelief. "Who are these people?" Kennedy once asked his cabinet. At the time, he meant President Achmed Sukarno and his Indonesian supporters, but he might as well have been asking about Japanese businessmen, Micronesian activists, or Australian conservatives. Kennedy and his colleagues, unable to see anything beyond their own power and technology, never succeeded in answering the basic questions concerning Asian/Pacific ambitions. Categorizing the needs and desires of various Asian/Pacific peoples under the simple heading of New Pacific Community was symbolic of the problem. The Kennedy administration wanted to consider Asian/Pacific development and security matters within a single, manageable framework. It was an impossible task, they soon discovered. The American government of the early 1960s grew as frustrated with Asian/Pacific politics as the Opium War-era British had been over a century earlier. They were agonizing over the problems of the "mysterious East," they said. By 1963, the enthusiasm of the New Frontiersmen had largely given way to confusion and doubt.

I am well aware of the perils involving the study of New Frontier diplomacy. Until recent years, many relevant documents have remained classified and the John F. Kennedy Library has been avoided by serious scholars because of it. Thanks to new declassifications and the helpful cooperation of the JFK Library staff, this account of JFK and his proposed New Pacific Community is possible. Nevertheless, there are still many limitations on the archival materials of the Kennedy presidency. While some collections simply require the former Cabinet or policy-maker's "permission for consultation," others remain mysteriously closed. The latter problem requires the researcher to investigate a variety of what, at first glance, appears to be records that are, at best, tangential to the tale. Often, these first impressions are mistaken and the so-called tangential records shed light on the reasons why some archival collections remain closed. Although an especially laborious task in contrast to research of the preceding presidencies, the Kennedy foreign policies do emerge for the researcher who refuses to give up the search. This study of the New Pacific Community is not the comprehensive work on US–Asian relations during the Kennedy era, nor does it pretend to be. Its aim involves the analysis of a critical phase in America's relationship with several areas of the Asian/Pacific region, and an examination of a Presidential administration's dream to leave a lasting American legacy there.

I offer my warmest thanks to the staff and directorship of the JFK Library, to the American Historical Association for its financial assistance to my research endeavors, and to my wife, Diana, for her patience, encouragement and critical reading of the manuscript in progress.

TIMOTHY P. MAGA

1 Finding the "Right Key:" Kennedy and the New Pacific Community

In 1958, William J. Lederer and Eugene Burdick offered a challenge to Kennedy's "new generation" soon to take power. As authors of the best-selling novel *The Ugly American*, Lederer and Burdick suggested that American policy in the Pacific region had divorced itself from American virtue. Since the Second World War, they stressed, America had demonstrated its greatness to the people of developing nations. Yet, American goodness had not been made clear to these same people. Indonesians, Filipinos, Australians, and others knew where America stood in the struggle "against" communism. But what was Washington "for"? America need not abandon its anti-communist mission, Lederer and Burdick argued, in order to achieve a happy, working relationship with the Third World. Wedding democratic and humanist virtue to Cold War diplomacy only required clever politics and an equally clever spokesman. The precise nature of the proposed policy of virtue was never important. Its promise was important, as well as the manner in which it was presented.

To Lederer and Burdick, championing the virtue of the "good America" always remained a tactic to achieve success in the anti-communist priorities of the "great America." Consequently, the best American representative in the Pacific region was one who knew how to "go off into the countryside and show the idea of America to the people. . . . Every person and every nation has a key which open their hearts. If you use the right key, you can maneuver any person or any nation any way you want."[1]

This message could not have been clearer to John Kennedy. Throughout his brief Presidency, he attempted to find "the right key" in the Asian/Pacific Third World. Indeed, at a time that coincided with the first publication of *The Ugly American*, the then Senator Kennedy struggled through a speech which called for a more humanist, caring America throughout the Pacific region. Speaking in Hawaii, Senator Kennedy advocated an effective challenge to

1

communist growth in the Pacific; a challenge based on a moral and democratic partnership with the Asian/Pacific states.

The people of the Pacific are not interested in being sold to the highest bidder. On the contrary, if our aid is given on the assumption that this will buy us friends, if they feel they are being made pawns in the Cold War, if they regard the United States only as a military guardian, a giver of goods or a lender of cash, then no amount of economic aid will strengthen our cause in that area.

Instead, we must return to the generous spirit; stress our positive interest in and moral responsibility for relieving misery and poverty; and acknowledge to ourselves and to the world that communism or no communism, we cannot be an island unto ourselves. We want the Pacific and America, with common ties and common concerns, to consider each other what they really are: partners in the world community.[2]

Kennedy ended his speech by praising the racial harmony embraced by his Hawaiian listeners, suggesting that racial harmony on the American mainland would best demonstrate the type of virtue and image that American policy must champion in the Pacific.[3] In short, he implied that a lessening of black-white tensions in America would also weaken the Soviet charge that many American policies were influenced by racist decisions. This speech was Kennedy's first and last public address on general Pacific policy until after his election as President. For the most part, it represented his noblest vision for the Pacific region; a vision that remained unchanged during his Presidency. Efforts to find the "right key" would complicate that vision.

In January 1961, Kennedy considered America's approach to Asian/Pacific policy worthy of a top-to-bottom review by his State Department. As in many areas of policy, Kennedy's requests for review carried immediate deadlines. Consequently, Kennedy's review and his decision on it were accomplished between late January and early April 1961.

During this period, and even before, the New Frontiersmen accused the so-called "tired men" of the Eisenhower administration of lacking patriotic ambition. To Kennedy and his colleagues, there had been several examples of Eisenhower's weakness in the face of Cold War challenges, especially in the Third World. In the cases of Indonesia, Egypt, and India, for instance, the Eisenhower administration, said the Kennedy team, had failed to address the issue of non-alignment. Indeed, John Foster Dulles, Eisenhower's Secretary of State, had considered non-alignment, or the Third World effort to maintain economically beneficial relations with the opposing sides of the Cold War, as *de facto* collaboration with communism. Dulles's CIA-sponsored endeavors to topple the Pacific's self-appointed spokesman for non-alignment, President Sukarno of Indonesia, illustrated the point in the late 1950s.

Despite Dulles's militant anti-communist rhetoric and use of the CIA in a coup against a non-alignment leader, the Kennedy administration pointed out that the Indonesia coup had failed and that Dulles's rhetoric always mentioned America's opposition to the growth of communism in the Third World but never mentioned what America should stand for there. This type of policy approach completed a circle of failure that was intolerable to the new Kennedy administration. Given the continued existence of non-alignment sentiment and the expansion of communism in Asia and even Cuba, the Kennedy team worried that time was running out to challenge America's ideological enemies effectively. Kennedy's inaugural invitation for Americans to assist him in the winning of the Cold War symbolized the post-World War II "can do" philosophy so prevalent within his generation's psyche. On the other hand, it also reflected Kennedy's own belief that the Eisenhower administration had squandered a certain opportunity to champion American goodness, impress the Third World, and deaden the appeal of communism to the downtrodden.

Eisenhower's Farewell Address appeared to confirm this latter conclusion. Whereas Eisenhower worried about a "military-industrial complex" and the impact of Cold War extremism in American life and politics, the new Kennedy administration considered the aging President's long goodbye speech a call to tone down the anti-communist crusade. Kennedy had nothing against Cold War extremism, only its proper direction. Breaking away from the Eisenhower-Dulles reliance on "bigger bang for the buck" nuclear diplomacy in favor of reliance on a diplomacy backed by both nuclear and conventional forces was part of that proper direction. Divorcing America from its "Ugly American" image and demonstrating democratic goodwill wherever possible remained more difficult to translate into policy, but the effort suggested anti-communist progress to the Kennedy administration and stood in contrast to the alleged Eisenhower retreat from the Cold War mission.

Paraphrasing Woodrow Wilson in his inaugural address, Kennedy suggested that American foreign policy had indeed lost its sense of mission. In 1913, Wilson, the first victorious Democratic Presidential candidate since the early 1890s, had offered support to a Republican President's (Teddy Roosevelt) precedent-setting "speak softly and carry a big stick" approach to diplomacy. That approach had implied a policy of global expansionism which included both traditional diplomacy and a powerful US Navy to champion America's burgeoning world power status. Wilson proclaimed that Roosevelt's efforts had not gone far enough. He spoke in general terms about his country's democratic responsibilities to the world, calling for a special, activist role for America in international affairs. His militant foreign policies from Haiti to Mexico suggested to many that he was obsessed with the idea of spreading American-styled democracy, even if the targeted countries were reluctant to accept it. His religious-like fervor in foreign policy-making won him the nicknames of "warrior priest" and "missionary diplomatist."

Authors such as Edward Buehrig, in his classic *Wilson's Foreign Policy in Perspective* (1957), warned future presidential candidates about the perils of diplomacy with "a sense of mission." Wilson's overly zealous foreign policy eventually stood in uncompromising opposition to Congress and public opinion leading to the president's downfall and the expansion of isolationist sentiment in the country. Later authors, such as James MacGregor Burns in his *Edward Kennedy and the Camelot Legacy* (1976), pointed out that John Kennedy and his two brothers in the late 1950s were well aware of the warnings offered by Buehrig and others. Leading a crusade in a foreign policy-making that did not enjoy the full support of the electorate would be disastrous for the Democratic Party, as had been the case following the collapse of the Wilson administration. It would also mean a quick end to the influence of the Kennedy brothers within that Party. Given John Kennedy's elevation of Wilson in his speeches, particularly Wilson's once rejected idea of a working world association of nations, it was obvious that he admired the late president's vision of avoiding conflict via international cooperation. Kennedy's own global vision welcomed the modern personification of Wilson's old idea, the United Nations, but he also admired the aggressive presidential style that Wilson demonstrated in unilateral foreign policy-making.

To Kennedy, there was a place for international dialogue and there was a place for American "guidance" of that dialogue. The trick was walking the fine line between the arrogance of power, or

Imperial Presidency, and popularly accepted strong leadership. The Eisenhower administration, Kennedy told a Pacific leadership conference in Hawaii during 1960, had embraced neither an arrogant foreign policy nor a strong, internationally popular one. America's foreign policy, he said, was "stagnant" in the Third World and especially in the Asian/Pacific region. Kennedy's simply stated vision of the President's role in global affairs accented the point.

When it came to the President's place as leader of the non-communist world, Kennedy insisted that he must be "in the thick of the fight, like Wilson at Versailles. He must care passionately about the fate of the people he leads, that he be willing to serve them at the risk of incurring their momentary displeasure." America and the President's world role in the 1960s, Kennedy explained, "consists of the combined purposefulness of each of us when we are at our moral best: striving, risking, choosing, making decisions, engaging in the pursuit of happiness that is strenuous, heroic, exciting, and exalted."[4] His comments were made with a sense of urgency, implying that he would be inheriting a losing position in the Cold War from the Eisenhower administration. This conclusion is essential to the understanding of the Kennedy foreign policy, for "special devices" would be required to win that Cold War. Fearing the collapse of Southeast Asia, the Kennedy team considered The New Pacific Community its most significant and elaborate "special device."

What does America hope to achieve in the Pacific? How can it win the allegiance of the Pacific Third World and also win the Cold War? What is happening in the areas near the Indochina conflict and how must America respond to problems there? These were the tough questions left to Kennedy's policy review team, the Policy Planning staff of the State Department. In the meantime, the young President continued to hint at the type of cooperative world framework that he would like to see established in the 1960s. During March 1961, while speaking to a group of Latin American diplomats about America's support for Third World economic development and social reform, Kennedy noted that "the efforts of governments alone will never be enough."

> In the end, the people must choose and the people must help themselves. . . . Let us once again transform the American continent into a vast crucible of revolutionary ideas and efforts – a tribute to the power of the creative energies of free men and

women – an example to all the world that liberty and progress
walk hand in hand.[5]

Be it in defense of hemispheric cooperation or Pacific partnership,
Kennedy offered high rhetoric. But he never achieved the goals that
he set. Capital investments in the Pacific and elsewhere remained
meager and his administration did little to stimulate private sector
interest in development projects. Moreover, the "creative energies"
that Kennedy touted in his March 1961 speech were more appropriately attributed to the communist movements within various Third
World nations. America's Third World allies rarely embraced the
political and economic reforms that Kennedy suggested in his
speeches.

The Kennedy administration's foreign policy decisions were often
marked by a struggle between visionary and practical policy considerations. Indeed, a common theme in Kennedy's foreign affairs
decisions was Presidential opposition to the repressive policies of
anti-communist allies in the Third World. Yet pressures to resolve
foreign policy crises usually forced him to ignore this opposition.
Many governments facing internal communist subversion in their
countries, Kennedy told the Congress in May 1961, also faced the
discontent of people who had been politically abused in the name of
anti-communism. "Military pacts," he stressed, "cannot help nations
whose social injustice and economic chaos invite insurgency and
penetration and subversion."[6] Two years later he told the press that
South Vietnam was one of those repressive allied nations. "We can
help them," Kennedy said of the Vietnamese, "we can give them
equipment, we can send our men out there as advisors, but they
have to win it, the people of Vietnam, against the Communists."[7]

It was to Kennedy's credit as a skillful politician and image-con-
scious President that his difficulty in combining vision with practical
policy concerns did not become an issue in the press or the public
mind. On the one hand, "the pay any price" Kennedy was always
ready to use "massive retaliation" to win the Cold War. On the
other hand, Kennedy's championing of social and economic reform
abroad indicated that the President was aware of the fact that many
people were not willing to "pay any price" on the behalf of governments that they did not support. Lasting peace and success for the
anti-communist cause depended upon what his cabinet called "the
winning of the hearts and minds" of foreign peoples.[8]

This dual approach to policy also remained a consistent one. Be it Cuba, Berlin, Indochina, or wherever the President considered American interests at stake, Kennedy warned his adversaries that American military power stood at the ready. Yet when hostilities drew near, he tried his best to avoid them and usually did. Thus, he also focused his efforts on forestalling crises and cultivating relations with areas adjacent to trouble spots, such as in what was soon to be called the New Pacific Community of Australia, Micronesia, Indonesia, the Philippines, Japan, and the Ryukyu Islands.

To early political and historical analysts of the Kennedy Presidency, such as Richard Walton, Kennedy's approach to policy was easy to explain. Writing in 1972, Walton accused Kennedy, in *Cold War and Counterrevolution: The Foreign Policy of John F. Kennedy*, of using alleged concern for world peace and harmony as a "smoke-screen." Kennedy's real ambition, he wrote, was American "domination" of the non-communist world. According to Walton, Kennedy was a militant conservative, and his talk of world peace and democratic reforms was utter nonsense.[9] To Ted Sorensen, a close Kennedy confidant and advisor, the dualism in the Kennedy approach to foreign relations was a positive development in policymaking. Dismissing "domination" as a goal of the Kennedy administration, Sorensen also rejected simple political labels, such as militant conservative, for his boss. Kennedy's approach to policy, Sorensen noted in his little known *Decision-Making in the White House*, was represented in the patriotic symbol of the American eagle in the presidential seal. Clasping arrows in one claw and olive branches in the other, the eagle, Sorensen pointed out, indicated the dual nature of the president's war-making and peace-making powers. Kennedy, he concluded, maintained an "even balance" of these powers.[10]

In fact, the Kennedy cabinet came to prefer arrows to olive branches.[11] Expecting victory in Vietnam, regardless of the policy it employed, the Kennedy administration always saw a golden opportunity to influence events in key areas throughout Vietnam's Asian/-Pacific neighborhood.

By April 1961, the State Department had completed its Presidentially-ordered study of America's relationship to the Asian/Pacific region. It was undertaken, Secretary Rusk explained to fellow cabinet members, in the interest of preventing a re-run elsewhere of the complicated Vietnam situation, and with the hope of finding some means to stimulate democratic and economic "progress" in "significant locations" throughout the Pacific. No specific event or diplomatic matter had compelled Kennedy to order this review. Particu-

larly in the early months of his administration, Kennedy preferred
to examine thoughtfully, but quickly, foreign policies that were taken
for granted by the Eisenhower administration. In short, he believed
that the world was a more complicated place than Eisenhower suggested. Its problems deserved greater reflection from a nation with
world responsibilities.[12] Nevertheless, Kennedy's confusion over
proper visionary and practical policies affected this basic conclusion.
His rapid approval of the Eisenhower-planned, CIA-led invasion of
Cuba at the Bay of Pigs did not represent the type of reflective,
analytical policy decisions that he otherwise championed.

Indeed, the State Department's Asia/Pacific policy review
coincided with the ill-fated Bay of Pigs operation. A special cabinet
meeting was called to discuss the study's recommendations. Admit-
ting that the study had been a difficult one, Secretary Rusk opened
the April 1961 meeting with the comment that the Pacific, in general,
posed special problems to American policy. The shape of the problem, he said, could be seen in the struggle of certain nations and
territories to reach a high stage of political/economic development.
His study had concentrated on Guam, the Trust Territory of the
Pacific Islands, Indonesia, Australia, Japan, the Ryukyu Islands, and
the Philippines.[13]

These nations, territories, and occupied islands, Rusk assured the
President, were not simply pulled out of a hat. There were reasons
for their stress in the study. Most of these reasons fell within two
contingencies. First, America must be ready to champion its victory
over the communists in Indochina by actively assuring other Asian/
Pacific locations of Washington's on-going commitment to peaceful
Third World development. Secondly, if American efforts in Indochina were bogged down, the United States would still have to
be ready to focus its "full attentions" on neighboring Asian/Pacific
locations. "Full attentions" meant shoring up strategic/defense ties
with specific nations and territories, as well as initiating new economic assistance programs.

Not surprisingly, the theme of the State Department review
reflected Kennedy's view of the Third World and the Pacific. The
State Department presented a scenario whereby certain areas of the
Asian/Pacific region were prisoners of the Cold War. The "side,"
American or Soviet, which appealed to these areas first would win
their allegiance and, therefore, win the Cold War in the Pacific.
Hence, the matter of reviving or "upgrading" American policy in
the Pacific remained a matter of successful "maneuvering" of select

governments. The Eisenhower administration, Rusk noted, preferred "raw confrontation" to "maneuvering." When it came to Pacific diplomacy, the Eisenhower White House, Rusk explained, "dealt with a real problem with unreal techniques drawing on questionable analogies."[14]

Considering the 'Pacific a "most vulnerable" area to communist penetration, Rusk noted that sufficient time and effort had been spent by Kennedy's predecessors to build an Asian/Pacific policy stressing Chiang Kai-Shek's Taiwan and Mao Tse-Tung's China. The former was secure, Rusk concluded, and the latter had been effectively isolated from world politics. A policy of vision was needed to include the "forgotten" but significant nations and territories of the region.

Japan, for instance, was one of these "forgotten" nations to be maneuvered in the interest of winning the Cold War. J. Robert Schaetzel, the State Department advisor and analyst who had prepared the study for Rusk, pointed out that no one nation or territory in his study required more urgent attention than the other. Rusk agreed. In the case of Japan, American–Japanese relations had reached a watershed. Japan's "exploding industrial society is vital to us," Rusk explained to his colleagues in the cabinet. "Because Japan is not closely associated with any Western entity other than the United States," Rusk recommended that Tokyo's interest in a healthy foreign trade relationship must be cultivated by the United States.[15]

With the position of the American military bases in Japan assured by treaty only months before Kennedy took office, the American government enjoyed a fine opportunity to downplay its lingering image in Japan as an occupying power. Although the American occupation had ended almost a decade earlier, the Japanese treaty of 1960 assured a continued presence by the America military. The specifics of the treaty had stimulated considerable anti-American sentiment throughout Japan. Rusk suggested that a new commitment to American–Japanese "economic cooperation" would extinguish this sentiment. It would also symbolize American friendship better than the Eisenhower stress on "joint American–Japanese distrust of the Soviet Union."[16] This happy, working relationship had been a goal of General Douglas MacArthur's occupation administration. Its time had come, the State Department's study suggested, promising that Japanese economic growth, enthusiastically supported and encouraged by the United States, would also meet the warm approval of Japan's Pacific trade partners.

Despite the glowing prediction of warm American–Japanese friendship and cooperation, there were specific matters that threatened it. One of the more controversial issues involved the future of the Ryukyu Islands directly to the south of Japan. Occupied by American forces following a series of bloody battles in 1945, the Ryukyus were also the home of Kadena Air Base, the Third Marine Division, and Torii Station Army base on the island of Okinawa. Japan claimed sovereignty over the island chain, while America preferred the security of occupation.

Hoping to defend their own unique culture, cultivate long-standing ties with Japan, yet take advantage of the American dollar, many Okinawans and other islanders hoped to play Washington off Tokyo. Rusk suggested that reason must prevail in this complicated issue of conflicting interests. Indeed, as long as the rights of the locals were protected and American basing rights assured, the return of Japanese sovereignty appeared to be the wisest policy. It could demonstrate to all Pacific residents that America desired to bury the World War II past and that it had no "imperial designs" in the region.

Demonstrating that American intentions were noble and not "ugly" in the Pacific remained at the heart of the State Department's study. The Kennedy cabinet was particularly sensitive to charges of "hypocrisy" and "colonial tyranny" levelled against it by the Soviet Premier, Nikita Khrushchev. Khrushchev had made these charges during a January 1961 speech directed against the new President and his alleged concern for international human rights. Khrushchev pointed out that the American-administered United Nations mandate over the Trust Territory of the Pacific Islands was the last of the post-World War II mandates still in existence. The Trust Territory, Khrushchev said, encompassed the size of the continental United States, and it remained the colonial preserve of Washington. How could Kennedy label Soviet policy imperialist, Khrushchev asked, when it was America that remained one of the world's most significant colonial powers? "Freedom to the American Pacific," Khrushchev exclaimed to the Western press.[17]

"If we are to succeed anywhere," Kennedy told his cabinet, "we must succeed in the Western Pacific."[18] To Kennedy, a World War II Pacific veteran, the Western Pacific was Micronesia, or the American territory of Guam and the Trust Territory. According to Rusk, if Washington "terminated" the United Nations mandate and placed both Guam and the Trust Territory on the road to statehood or some other "permanent association" with the United States, the Khrushchev charges would be answered. More significantly, the image of the caring, noble America would be easier to champion throughout the Pacific region. To an extent, Khrushchev was right. The American presence in Micronesia carried embarrassingly strong colonial overtones in an era of Pacific decolonization. Boldly assuming that the islanders desired closer ties to the United States, Kennedy predicted statehood for the Micronesian islands by 1970.

The nearby former American colony of the Philippines presented yet another challenge to Rusk and his policy review. Whereas Micronesia suggested a coming era of political and economic growth to the State Department, the Philippines appeared to be in a state of political and economic chaos. The problem might not be remedied by 1960, Rusk announced, but, in the meantime, America could assure a secure presence for its large naval and air forces presence there by stepping up its economic and military munitions program. The Philippines still enjoyed a "competent infrastructure," Rusk noted, to support political and economic growth. All it needed was "further stimulus" from the United States. To the Kennedy cabinet, this "stimulus" would symbolize America's commitment to development in struggling Third World nations. Indeed, the image of the former colonial master, helping the decolonized help themselves, was attractive to Kennedy. He asked his cabinet to seek support in Congress for a dramatic boost in foreign aid to the Philippines. But would the Philippines use the aid appropriately? Although he worried about the answer, Kennedy still favored aid.

Finally, there was the problem of Achmed Sukarno of Indonesia. Like the Philippines, Indonesia presented several difficulties to the Kennedy team in the realm of political and economic development. In contrast to the Philippines, Indonesia's problems were of a more serious, immediate concern to Kennedy. Obviously, there were areas in the Pacific, despite Rusk and Schaetzel's original opinion, that required urgent attention. Sukarno's government welcomed elements of the strong Communist Party of Indonesia (PKI) within it. Moreover, Sukarno's "Guided Democracy" rejected American-styled democracy, justifying strong-armed rule and a foreign policy of non-alignment. As Indonesia's most famous hero in the war of liberation against the Japanese and then the Dutch, Sukarno remained the symbol of stability in his impoverished nation. If Sukarno fell victim to a coup, retired, or died, Rusk warned Ken-

nedy, the Indonesian leader's power base would be inherited by the
PKI.

Dealing with Sukarno would never be easy, Rusk predicted. The
charismatic Indonesian leader enjoyed wide respect throughout Southeast Asia. The Eisenhower administration's efforts to topple him
in an unsuccessful CIA-sponsored plot in 1958 only led to Sukarno's
entrenchment, worsening Washington's "ugly American" image in
the Pacific. Rusk recommended a "meaningful dialogue" with
Sukarno in the interest of: (1) stimulating economic development in
Indonesia; (2) impressing all of Southeast Asia with America's peaceful intentions; and (3) assuring American economic interests in
Indonesian oil, tin, and rubber. If successful in this difficult proving
ground, the winning of Pacific region allegiances to the American
side in the Cold War might be quickly achieved. Hence, preventing
communist growth in Indonesia soon became as important as halting
its more violent expression in Vietnam.[19]

Kennedy appreciated the advice and encouragement from his State
Department. The direction and significance of it all remained unclear
to him until Secretary Rusk provided a working framework for success. Concluding his review for the cabinet, Rusk promised that the
problems associated with the specific areas noted in his study could
be "managed."[20] The management effort would stress a new mini-
version of the United Nations. Called the New Pacific Community,
this organization would not conflict with the work of existing international organizations. Its role would be to plan and coordinate
the economic development of the Pacific region as well as oppose
communist growth.

The locations noted in Rusk's study would play primary roles in
the directing body of the organization. Essentially acting as referees,
American representatives would always be present at New Pacific
Community meetings. Rusk recommended Australia as its headquarters. The Australians, he pointed out, were the most successful,
American-styled democrats in the Pacific region. With America's
help, Australia could become the symbol of the best possible Pacific
state, championing America's view of economic development and
peace throughout the Pacific.

Although American–Australian relations were warm, Rusk was
not pleased with Canberra's reluctance to become involved in anti-
communist causes, particularly in Southeast Asia. Australia would
be flattered by its American-deemed "activist role" in the new organization, Rusk believed. It was only a matter of time, he said, before

Canberra accepted its destiny as America's anti-communist partner in the Pacific.[21]

The precise mechanics as to how the organization would be established, administered, and financed was not discussed in the spring of 1961. For the moment, the Kennedy cabinet congratulated itself on creating a scenario to solve the problems of the Pacific. They proceeded as if the details to this grand plan would fall into place later. The vision remained more important than practical policy. Moreover, this path to policy-making was not taken because the issues were less important than Berlin, Cuba, or some other headline-maker in foreign affairs. American influence in the Pacific remained an important matter to the Kennedy administration.[22]

Despite the careful gathering of mounds of data and its manipulation by skilled minds, the conclusions to the State Department's Pacific policy review were largely based on bold assumptions and patriotic ambitions. No one could disagree with the Kennedy administration's desire for peace, development, and security in the Pacific. On the other hand, its method in achieving this goal promised to remain immensely complicated, forcing developing countries and territories to submit to the whims of America, the donor-aid nation. For over two years, the White House would fail to understand why the New Pacific Community Proposal was not welcomed enthusiastically in the Pacific. Was there something wrong with America's vision for the Pacific? Did American power have limits? Kennedy's New Pacific Community encouraged these questions. The young President had no answers.

2 Rust Removal: the New Frontier in Guam and the Trust Territory of the Pacific Islands

Planting the seeds of a lasting and positive American legacy in the Pacific remained a mammoth task for the Kennedy team. For all effective purposes, Kennedy considered his New Pacific Community policy a revision of the longstanding anti-communist mission in the Pacific and what it hoped to accomplish there. Given his concern over image, both his own and his country's, as well as his concern over the successful development of anti-communist institutions overseas, Kennedy had ambitious plans for the American Pacific. Guam and the Trust Territory of the Pacific Islands constituted a unique case in the New Pacific Community vision. Guam's constitutional status as a United States Territory and the American-administered United Nations Trusteeship over the northern Mariana, Caroline, and Marshall Islands created certain responsibilities for the United States.[1] Had America offered these areas adequate administration and political guidance? What was their future in the face of an increasingly volatile Pacific? Was there substance to Khrushchev's charge of abuse and neglect? In light of the New Pacific Community, the potential answers to these questions intrigued Kennedy.

The symbolism was strong. If America could offer what amounted to a New Deal to its own Pacific wards, and have that New Deal welcomed by the islanders, Washington would establish a foundation for success in anti-communist and Third World development causes throughout the non-American Pacific. Washington would clean its own house, the American Pacific, demonstrating the strength of its new commitment to peaceful change and development. Symbolism was always important to the Kennedy team, and the challenge of answering Khrushchev's charges remained an exciting one.

By 1961, Guam and the Trust Territory of the Pacific Islands had become the forgotten "province" of the American empire. Most Americans associated the exotic tropical island chains of the Marianas, Carolines, and Marshalls with haunting memories of World War II battles. It was an area, according to the Truman and Eisenhower administrations, worth forgetting. In the 1950s, the American government maintained only one consistent and successful policy in the Western Pacific islands; reducing the budget. This approach left no funds for repairing the Quonsets and vehicles inherited from the navy following World War II. Aircraft still landed in lagoons for lack of runways. The education system focused only on the needs of the dependent children of American military personnel stationed there, and local political concerns received scant recognition from Washington. In January 1961, Delmas Nucker, the United States High Commissioner of the Pacific Trust Territory, informed the Insular Affairs Subcommittee of the House of Representatives that no changes were planned or needed for the coming year and decade. All was well in paradise.[2]

John Kennedy disagreed with Nucker's assessment. Publicly vowing to extend his New Frontier programs to Micronesia, Kennedy announced that his administration had both a "moral and political responsibility" to rescue what he nicknamed the "Rust Territories," as well as Guam, from further decay.[3] For over two years, he attempted to make good this promise, and with an aggressiveness that astonished even the islanders. To a large degree, Micronesia became a microcosm of what Kennedy hoped to achieve at home. Congress and the press paid little attention to Micronesian politics and events. Hence, the ultra-caution that characterized Kennedy's approach to civil rights and other controversial issues on the mainland could be discarded in Micronesia. He enjoyed a fine opportunity to extend civil rights/civil liberties benefits to the islanders and never fear a political backlash. Without worrying about extended Congressional debate or significant opposition, he could also offer an economic aid program, courting the full involvement of the islanders in its administration. In short, the issues of racial equality and economic development could be easily focused there, creating the first quick success for the New Frontier. The key to that success was a fast-acting Washington that encouraged the interaction of islanders, development experts, and federal officials in the name of economic progress, racial harmony, and, most likely, statehood.[4]

Although his plans for Micronesia in 1961 remained a mixture of statehood visions and financial authorization requests from Congress, Kennedy described his efforts to extend the New Frontier to the islands as exciting and challenging.[5] No President had attached those terms to Micronesian policy before. It had always been a backwater to American global interests. Kennedy's desire to establish the New Pacific Community only partially explained his enthusiasm. Wayne Aspinall, Chairman of the House Committee on Interior and Insular Affairs during the early 1960s, once labeled Kennedy's Pacific island concerns "obsessive." The President, he said, always remembered his war years in the Pacific when the topic of Micronesia was raised. During World War II, Kennedy had been disturbed by the primitive living conditions of Pacific islanders. Nearly twenty years later, the new President wanted to "lead the American Pacific islands into the twentieth century," Aspinall explained. It was an unfinished chore of the allied victory in World War II, and Kennedy, Aspinall reasoned, thought he had inherited this task.[6]

Aspinall's matter-of-fact explanation for Kennedy's personal interest in Micronesian affairs remains the only known account by a policy-maker. Whether "obsessed" or simply concerned, Kennedy was attracted to Micronesian issues, and this fact was unique for a Massachusetts-based politician. Even the Hawaiian delegation in Congress expressed little interest in nearby Micronesian developments.

Despite the interest, Kennedy was confused over the issues at hand in Micronesia. Viewing the Pacific islands as a geographic whole, Kennedy assumed that there was little difference between the slow pace of political/economic development in the American Pacific versus the British-administered islands to the south. In fact, Kennedy had never visited Guam and the future Trust Territory during his war years. He assumed that Pacific islanders, regardless of location, were victims of colonial-inspired white racism, and that their political/economic prowess was weak.[7] The former assumption was based on what he observed as a navy officer stationed in the Solomon islands of the South Pacific during World War II. Ironically, the latter assumption was based on the type of racial assessment that he hoped to eliminate. Like the many American politicians of his era, and the many that succeeded him, Kennedy thought that economic/political conditions on Guam were the same or similar on Saipan in the Northern Marianas, Ponape in the Carolines, or Majuro in the Marshalls. He was wrong.

Kennedy's concern for Micronesia first became known to the public during the 1958 Senate debate over Hawaii statehood. Creating the state of Hawaii, Kennedy said, would help turn America's attentions toward current events in the other Pacific possessions.

It will help, I am hopeful, all Americans to take a new look at our responsibilities in that area, and to have a better understanding of the peoples of those areas, their needs and aspirations. For these islands are the ideal example of how Asia and America, East and West, can meet together on free and equal terms. . . . If we can demonstrate a real concern, if we can spend a small sum that may save us billions later, then our task will be easier and our future more secure.[8]

As an unsuccessful contender for the Democratic Party's Vice Presidential nomination in 1956, a Massachusetts Senator, and an undeclared candidate for President in 1960, Kennedy, by 1958, already had a strong platform to voice his concerns on a variety of issues. Yet, his influence on these issues was questionable, mostly because his Senate attendance record during the late 1950s remained poor, and because his quest for the Presidency often dominated his approach to all issues. It was remarkable that a certain curiosity over the future of the Pacific islands could survive this quest, but his interest had apparently taken root in 1943.

During August 1943, following the ramming of his PT–109 by a Japanese destroyer in Blackett Strait west of New Georgia, Kennedy owed his life and eventual rescue to Pacific islanders; a fact that he never forgot. The episode made him reflect on the tranquility of Pacific island life upset by war, and on war itself. On 12 September 1943, he wrote to his parents, that his months in the Pacific would have a lasting impact on his life.

When I read that we will fight the Japs for years if necessary and will sacrifice hundreds of thousands if we must – I always like to check from where he is talking – it's seldom out here [Pacific islands]. People get too used to talking about billions of dollars and millions of soldiers that thousands of dead sound like a drop in the bucket. But if those thousands want to live as much as the ten [PT–109 crewmen] I saw – they should measure their words with great, great care.[9]

By 1961, Kennedy's desire to provide a caring, praiseworthy policy for the United States Pacific was part of his larger vision of a more racially harmonious, forward-moving America by 1970 or 1980. Athough written by his Senate staff, the Kennedy-attributed 1956 work, *Profiles in Courage*, outlined the Kennedy view of heroic policy. As President John Quincy Adams had suggested in the 1820s.

Profiles in Courage implied that a federally-supported and encouraged public education could eliminate racism within a generation's time. Moreover, Secretary of State John Quincy Adams implied in his writing of President Monroe's famous Doctrine that a nation which cared for its international safety, as well as for the welfare of its neighbors, demonstrated both its greatness and humanity.

Obviously, Kennedy and his staff admired Adams's sense of noble mission, particularly in the realm of ending racism and championing American responsibilities *vis-à-vis* neighboring, developing areas. The sixth President of the United States played a significant role in *Profiles in Courage*, and his views on the American government's potential impact on generational change represented an important part of the book's thesis.[10] Abandoning America's neglectful Micronesian policy in favor of new, progressive measures could be seen as a manifestation of the *Profiles in Courage* thesis.[11] Defining those measures was a different matter, however. Kennedy continued to have a difficult time translating what were often academic-styled theses into policy. Aside from matters of Cold War and New Pacific Community propaganda, did Micronesia need civil rights and political/economic reforms? Without consulting island leaders, Kennedy concluded that something done was better than nothing at all.[12]

Guam appeared to be the most logical location to achieve the swiftest and happiest results for Kennedy's New Pacific Community reforms.[13] A prize of the Spanish-American War, Guam had been administered by a navy regime until the Japanese invasion and occupation of December 1941. Located some 1400 miles east of Manila, this 32-mile long island had been surrounded in a Japanese sea since 1914. In that year, Japan had defeated the German empire in Micronesia, and in 1919 it received a League of Nations mandate to administer the former German colonies in the Marianas, Carolines, and Marshall island chains.

Settled in islands stretching from Palau in the Carolines directly south of Guam, to Majuro in the Marshalls only 2,000 miles from Hawaii, the Japanese had entertained adventurous plans to modernize their Pacific empire; however, World War II intervened. After the war, Guam returned to American navy rule, but after much protest from the native Chamorros, the navy disbanded its government, permanent residents became American citizens, and a territorial government was established in 1950. The Department of the Interior won Guam under its jurisdiction, and the President reserved the right to appoint the Governor. Meanwhile, the United States inherited the prewar Japanese Pacific empire. The American government received the authority from the United Nations, the reformed successor to the League of Nations, to create the Trust Territory of the Pacific Islands and to administer the former Japanese Pacific empire in the best interests of the United Nations. In reality, the United Nations simply confirmed the American presence in the region and ignored the colonial overtones.[14]

With the beginning of the Korean War, America's military attentions turned away from the old Pacific island battlegrounds and more directly towards the Asian continent. From Kwajalein in the Marshalls to Palau in the Carolines, World War II era military bases were slimmed down or closed in favor of increasing the military presence in Japan and Okinawa. The only exception remained Guam. Having proved its worth in the air war against Japan in 1945, the island became the home of Andersen Air Force Base in 1952.

In addition to its shrinking military significance, the Trust Territory also became of limited socio-economic value to Washington during the 1950s. For instance, whereas $500,000 was once targeted for "twentieth century" improvement to primary and secondary education in the Trust Territory during the early 1950s, by 1960 these funds had never been spent. In fact, only $9,164 was budgeted for 1960. Denouncing Truman's $500,000 plan as too ambitious and expensive, the Eisenhower administration argued that mainland-style public schools would destroy the traditional influence of the family in island education. Many islanders feared that the consequences of this decision would be devastating to the future of the region's youth.[15]

In all economic matters, mainland businesses were prohibited from establishing a foothold in the islands. The Governor of Guam, usually a Department of the Interior official, and the High Commissioner of the Trust Territory, usually a former Defense or State Department official, feared that new competition would wipe out struggling local businesses. Considering the economic boom on the American mainland in the 1950s, this policy assured that the islanders would remain divorced from the mainland economic successes. Finally, tight security restrictions still remained in Guam and all the islands, discouraging travelers to the region from the American mainland and elsewhere, as well as halting the dissemination of new ideas and information. The Navy Department insisted on these measures, including censorship, because the region's defenses remained the weakest of the Pacific command. Throughout the 1950s, the navy's concerns still had a primary influence on Pacific island policy, particularly in the Trust Territory, where, in contrast to Guam, the navy assisted in government administration. The navy's desire to remain a powerful element in local policy-making stemmed mostly from reasons of navy pride and the conviction that the Micronesians needed a firm hand in government.[16]

As far as the islanders were concerned, most of the disagreements between themselves and the American government authorities over matters of education, economics, and security fell under the general headings of isolation or colonial paternalism. The islanders' complaints were not transcended into organized political protests or parties of opposition. They remained more in the realm of angry opinion and in the hope that some political figure in Washington might offer a change of policy. Kennedy presented himself as that figure.[17] It was not until January 1961 that the future of America's Pacific possessions was studied by a Presidential administration. The original suggestion of a policy review, however, came from Joseph Flores, the Governor of Guam, and not Kennedy. Coinciding with the Kennedy cabinet's New Pacific Community discussions, Flores's suggestion was well-taken.

Flores, the publisher-editor of the *Guam Daily News* and *Territorial Sun*, had been appointed Governor by President Eisenhower shortly before the 1960 election. He was the first Guamanian to hold the post and he stood as a symbol to anyone who favored decolonization of the American Pacific. On 21 January 1961, Flores sent a message of praise to the newly inaugurated President, reminding him that his eloquent inaugural promise to extend "new frontiers" of peace and progress must include Micronesia. Kennedy's inaugural address was devoted almost entirely to foreign affairs, underscoring the perilous Cold War confrontation with the Soviet Union. His most quoted words, "Let us never negotiate out of fear. But let us never fear to negotiate" indicated that he would seek to alleviate international tensions in a peaceful fashion. Speaking for all of Micronesia, Flores asked Kennedy to ease tensions in the Pacific islands, stressing the point that security restrictions must be lessened in favor of free movement and the establishment of new businesses. Like the black Americans who supported the hopes and dreams of the incoming administration, Pacific Americans, Flores concluded, suffered from discrimination. Micronesia's future was inhibited by military priorities and aging executive orders. The

Governor urged that Kennedy review the situation and honor his promise of "new frontiers."[18]

In many respects, Flores's appeal was as eloquent as Kennedy's. But, at least one member of Kennedy's cabinet interpreted the Governor's message as a stern warning. Robert McNamara, the Secretary of Defense, welcomed the policy review suggestion, but he also considered Flores a troublemaker who might lead a movement of civil unrest behind America's line of anti-communist defense in the Far East. This would make a mockery of the American government's desire to maintain a certain solidarity among Pacific peoples against communist tyranny. To McNamara, Flores's appeal even suggested that the Pacific islanders might turn towards radical ideologies, such as communism, if they failed to get what they wanted.

Kennedy disagreed with McNamara's inference that the Pacific islanders were ready to embrace communism. Like Flores, Kennedy obviously saw the issue of Micronesian progress as part of the larger issues of world decolonization and racial equality.[19] By February 1961, Khrushchev had improved on his earlier attacks against American colonialism. He accused Kennedy of being hypocritical in his support for civil rights and European decolonization, noting that Jim Crow laws even applied to visiting Asian and African diplomats to the United States, and that America would "always" maintain its colonial "stranglehold" on the Pacific. Khrushchev's attacks were not unusual, but they were untimely to the American President. In the Western Pacific, Kennedy explained to McNamara during February 1961, the time had come to stop "playing Viceroy." That decision, he said, was long overdue.[20] Nevertheless, he did agree with McNamara that the Republican Flores was the wrong man to spearhead the New Frontier in Guam and the Trust Territory. The Governor must be considered the President's personal agent in the region, he said, championing a program of rapid change. A reliable mainland Democrat was needed until the struggling and small group of Guamanian Democrats could agree on local leadership issues. The President's interest implied that, under different circumstances, such as retirement, he would take the assignment himself. This, according to the future governor, was indeed the case. Kennedy instructed James Murray, Chairman of the Senate Committee on Interior and Insular Affairs, to begin hearings on Flores's replacement.[21]

The President's approach raised two questions here. First of all, given Kennedy's patrician lifestyle, it remained unlikely that he would retire to tiny Guam after his Presidency. It did suggest that the 43-year-old President did not plan to retire from political life, however. Most likely, he would follow the precedent that was set by John Quincy Adams and return to the House of Representatives. This type of speculation would continue throughout his years in the White House. His early remarks to Murray indicated that he also encouraged such discussions.

The second question raised by the Flores matter concerned the nature of Kennedy's approach to Micronesia itself. Although Flores's comments were generally welcomed by the Kennedy cabinet as a call to action, the Republican governor was fired shortly afterwards. Obviously, reform in Micronesia was going to be a personally championed policy by Kennedy and his team. Efficiency and results would be more valuable to the locals, they believed. Flores and his Republican friends would be quickly forgotten.[22]

The President's instructions confused Murray's committee. On the one hand, Kennedy spoke of racial equality and opening new doors of opportunity in the Western Pacific. On the other hand, he sought a stock political appointment to Guam. Senator Oren Long of Hawaii complained that replacing Flores with a mainlander would be a mistake, resulting in cries of racism and colonialism from Pacific islanders and even Asians. Kennedy dismissed the argument and maintained a steady course. To Kennedy, the appointment of a mainland New Frontiersman, preferably someone close to the Kennedy family and a Pacific war veteran, would be the first step in a modernization program that would spread from Guam to the remote islands of the Trust Territory. During the opening days of the administration, that program remained undefined; however, the need for one was clearly recognized. Flores was seen as an unnecessary burden from the Eisenhower years. Already frustrated in dealing with a politically divided Congress, Kennedy had no desire to leave in office a potentially troublesome Republican when he enjoyed the opportunity to replace him. The new appointee, Kennedy promised the people of Guam, would have open access to the President's office and would share his "deep commitment for change." Privately, Kennedy thought that his appointee would have a better chance than Flores in allaying the local military's fears once the old security restrictions were lifted. The islanders, he assured the House of Representatives and the Senate, will welcome their President's action as a sign of great things to come. Besides, he predicted that he would appoint a Guamanian-born Governor as early as 1962.[23]

In April 1961, William Daniel, a close friend of the Secretary of the Interior, Stewart Udall, and an acquaintance of the President, was appointed Governor of Guam and approved by Senator Murray's Committee. To the surprise of Senator Long, Flores, and others, Kennedy's assessment was proven correct. Daniel's appointment was greeted with enthusiasm in Guam and throughout the Trust Territory. Before leaving Government House overlooking Agana, the principal city of Guam, Flores sent a petition to the President calling for the revoking of Executive Order No. 8683, a measure dating to 14 February 1941, which granted the navy full control over the movement of vessels, businesses, information, and people to and from the American Western Pacific islands.[24] The only American-inhabited Western Pacific island in 1941 was Guam, and the considerations which compelled the establishment of security restrictions were irrelevant to the islanders of 1961. Reeling from the Bay of Pigs episode, Kennedy accepted the petition without public comment. It was Governor Daniel at his 20 May 1961 inaugural who stirred the islanders with the promise that more than action on one petition or a single Executive Order was in the offing.

We know that the United States has not done the best possible job. Our performance in this part of the world – Guam and the Trust Territory – now endure the scrutiny of the whole world – the free, the uncommitted and the enslaved. The Government of the United States cannot be a neutral in the drama of advancement in this area. We will be judged according to success or failure in achieving the self-sufficiency so essential to true freedom.[25]

During the early summer of 1961, the Kennedy administration began to concentrate its attentions on turning New Frontier rhetoric into reality. An 83 percent approval rating by the American people in the Gallup Poll buoyed the President's spirits in his handling of foreign affairs. On the other hand, his calling up of reserves during the Berlin Crisis in July 1961 worried Americans as the Cold War became warmer, and the sending of 400 United States marshalls to protect Freedom Riders in Montgomery, Alabama accented the growing racial tensions in the country. Kennedy proceeded cautiously with the priority issues of American–Soviet relations and civil rights. Indeed, some suggest that his caution reflected a fear of "personal" rejection of his New Frontier idealism by the American people.[26] It was in this atmosphere of caution and concern that Kennedy created his Micronesia policy. In spite of all the misfortunes that might befall his administration, Kennedy explained to Jose Benitez, the Deputy High Commissioner to the Trust Territory of the Pacific Islands, he would succeed in Micronesia.[27]

First of all, Kennedy planned to rescind Executive Order No. 8683 and two subsequent Orders that defended the military's special rights in the Pacific islands. Considering his growing concern and involvement in Southeast Asian politics, the lessening of American security restrictions in the Western Pacific appeared contradictory to other regional defense decisions. For instance, he approved a top secret military study (CENTPAC/WESTPAC, 1961) that planned to increase the military personnel of the Marianas islands, particularly on Guam and Saipan. The most controversial aspect of the study was the proposal to stock Andersen Air Force Base with nuclear weapons, and, in general, to build a nuclear strike task force in the Pacific islands. This study assumed that a major military effort in Southeast Asia was inevitable. Speaking for the navy at a cabinet discussion on Micronesia, Captain W. S. Sampson stressed the point that removing the security umbrella over the Western Pacific islands was a contradiction to the findings of the Presidentially inspired CENTPAC/WESTPAC study. More restrictions on Micronesian life would be in order.[28] Kennedy disagreed with all of Sampson's points, but as a conciliatory gesture to the navy, he promised to lift the Executive Orders under a six-month trial basis. The military, he said, had nothing to fear from the Pacific islanders or from democracy. It could only benefit the creation of a New Pacific Community.[29]

As soon as the Executive Order matter was resolved, Kennedy planned to move on three other issues. One included legislation to create the position of Territorial Delegate from Guam to the House of Representatives. Another involved the removing of the navy from any policy role in the Trust Territory, and physically moving the reformed Trust Territory administration and its headquarters from Guam in the southern Marianas to Saipan in the northern Marianas. The last issue involved the commissioning of a year long Presidential mission to the islands to study problems in economic development and mainland-island relations. Kennedy planned to act immediately on the mission's report.

The purpose of all this activity was open to much speculation in the islands and elsewhere after Kennedy announced his intentions in September 1961. Reflecting both island and Trust Territory opinion, the *Micronesian Reporter* believed that Kennedy was simply extending the New Frontier generosity to their homes; however, the matter was, of course, more complicated.[30] The State Department kept Kennedy informed of the *Micronesian Reporter*'s growing praise for the New Frontier, using it as an example of the type of Pacific solidarity required to face the communist challenge in Southeast Asia. America is decolonizing, Rusk proclaimed. Lengthy memoranda were also written to Kennedy on the propaganda value of the shift in Pacific island policy.[31]

The Central Intelligence Agency countered the State Department argument, adding fuel to McNamara's concern over communist influence in the American Pacific. Since 1949, the CIA had maintained a secret training base in northern Saipan. Disguised as the Naval Technical Training Unit (NTTU), this small base was used for the training of Chinese Nationalists from Taiwan to infiltrate mainland China. Since Saipan was part of the Trust Territory of the United Nations, the CIA base violated the United Nations Territorial Charter which denounced covert operations involving the islands. Whenever United Nations officials visited Saipan, CIA operatives, with the assistance of Navy Intelligence personnel, "sanitized" NTTU, making it appear like the usual jumble of Quonset huts that characterized the small bases of the Pacific. In a special report to the President, the NTTU complained that a shift in Micronesian policy would destroy their cover. The future of the region was grim, the CIA predicted. Thoughts on Asian nationalism and new ideas on racial pride from the American mainland would combine in the islands, resulting in a bloody uprising against American rule.

Apparently bitter over the Bay of Pigs episode, whereby anti-communist refugees were trained by the CIA and landed in Cuba, Kennedy offered a terse response to the NTTU. He noted that the Trust Territory headquarters would soon be moved from Guam to Saipan. Consequently, he expected the NTTU to be closed by the time of the public announcement of the transfer, and he ordered its operations disbanded.[32] From all accounts, Kennedy welcomed most of the official advice on Micronesia, but, as he once explained to Wayne Aspinall, the Defense Department and CIA sometimes missed the point. Washington must improve the health, education and welfare of the people in Guam and the Trust Territory, he told Aspinall, "because it is the right thing to do."[33] Although he never publicly announced that statehood for Micronesia was a goal of his administration, he implied to both Aspinall and Antonio B. Won Pat, Speaker of the Guam Legislature and future Delegate to the

House of Representatives, that just as man would walk the moon by 1970, Micronesia would soon win its star in the American flag.[34]

During the early 1960s, the Micronesians had basic infrastructure needs in mind, and not statehood. Nevertheless, the suggestion gave Kennedy a certain balance to his attacks on the status quo in the region, and caught his critics in the navy and elsewhere off guard. Meanwhile, Kennedy proceeded with his agenda. Events moved quickly. As a Christmas 1961 gift to the people of Guam and the Trust Territory, Kennedy lifted all Executive Orders which placed security restraints on island life. John B. Connally, the Secretary of the Navy, requested that this new era of openness be placed on the promised six-month trial basis. Kennedy agreed, but privately told Stewart Udall that he had no intention of restoring the Executive Orders. By January 1962, Connally realized that this was the case. He appealed to Kennedy to go slow in transferring the Trust Territory headquarters to Saipan and removing the navy from its policy-making role in that government.[35] In a polite gesture to the navy's pride, Kennedy granted the request, and, indeed, the formal transfer of full power to the civilian Trust Territory officials (mostly Department of Interior employees by 1962) was not made until June 1962. In reality, however, a working Department of Interior-guided government was established several weeks earlier, and a special United Nations mission, encouraged by the President had assisted in the endeavor. NTTU was closed by January 1962.[36]

Following the headquarters transfer, Kennedy ordered a task force to Micronesia consisting of representatives from the Bureau of the Budget, Department of the Interior, and Health, Education and Welfare. Each Department was expected to review those areas in its own field of competence. An even more comprehensive Presidential mission was to follow, acting on the findings of the task force. HEW reported that the islands needed to be "introduced to the twentieth century"; a task that it welcomed with enthusiasm. The Interior Department quipped in its conclusion that Eskimos enjoyed a warmer relationship with white America than Pacific islanders. A supreme effort was needed to integrate island communities. And the Bureau of the Budget noted that HEW's and Interior's plans would cost fourteen to fifteen million dollars. Kennedy accepted the latter figure and introduced legislation to that effect for fiscal year 1963. Congress honored his request as they did his legislation to welcome a Guam Delegate to the House of Representatives, a bill to provide for the economic rehabilitation of Guam, and the Guam urban renewal bill.[37]

Typical of the New Frontier, Kennedy's legislative efforts offered monetary incentives for the benefit of everything from Micronesian harbor extension projects to a new clinic in Palau. The precise mechanics of infrastructure assistance and its administration was never Kennedy's concern. In terms of budgets and even glowing rhetoric, the Micronesian component of the New Pacific Community vision never equalled the "Alliance for Progress" in Latin America, for instance. The New Pacific Community was an idea yet to be fully tested as late as 1963. On the other hand, Kennedy could claim "great beginnings" in alleviating poverty and bringing economic progress to Micronesia.[38]

Positive reaction to the "Let us begin" approach in the islands was important to Kennedy and the New Pacific Community idea. Arthur Dellinger, a California-born accountant and development expert, offered the type of reaction Kennedy desired. Having spent much of his adult life on Guam, Dellinger had been a longtime critic of Washington's neglect of Micronesia. He especially enjoyed the loyal support of Guam's small business community. In August 1962, Dellinger switched from virulent attack to praise for American policy, claiming that he represented the sentiments of a majority of Guamanian businessmen and concerned local citizens. The Kennedy administration saw this as a magnificent development and reprinted some of Dellinger's comments for the benefit of the Asian/Pacific embassies in Washington as well as for Members of Congress.

> The millions of people of the Philippine Islands, Indonesia, and of the Malayan Peninsula will take especial note of your progressive move. With respect to those Pacific or Asian areas which are either Communist-dominated or Communist-influenced, this is Democracy thrust at their throats, the only language they understand.
>
> The freedom of movement created by the Presidential Orders will undoubtedly bring to Guam and to the "Territory," the advent of much desired tourism. Much has been discussed about some of us Americans who are "ugly." Our next job, Mr. President, yours and mine, is to invite our fellow Americans out there and implore them to open their eyes and not be "ugly," because we Guamanians are proud that we now may be permitted to show what we

have to offer. I am confident that, of those who find their way out there, none will be disappointed.[39]

Such publicity efforts were not lost on the American press. Correspondents from *The New York Times*, ABC-News, and *U. S. News and World Report* covered the opening of the new Trust Territory headquarters on Saipan. Micronesia had not received mainland press attention since World War II, and one reporter, A. M. Rosenthal of *The New York Times*, entitled his first article, "Mike Who?" The press found a local populace that was receptive to the young President's concern but, in spite of presidential decrees and legislative efforts, little had changed in the islands.[40]

Strik Yoma, a resident of Ponape and a 1962 Fellow at Hawaii's East-West Center, offered an eloquent and objective account of the Micronesian reaction to Kennedy. Yoma was not courted by the visiting press. Indeed, the latter remained more interested in finding examples of Kennedy grandeur than analyzing the Micronesian story. Publishing in the *Micronesian Reporter*, Yoma praised the Kennedy administration's interest in a matter that brought, as far as he could determine, little economic and political benefit to the American mainland. Yoma's praises for Kennedy ended here, and his concerns, unheard in Washington, were more reflective of majority opinion than Dellinger's. Yoma believed that specific economic assistance programs to the struggling fish and coconut tree industries would have won quicker and greater support for the President. These specific programs to the island's two major industries were not entertained by the Kennedy administration. Why not, he wondered? The local economic benefit from such programs would eventually translate into islander-run infrastructure development projects. Wasn't local control of development matters a goal of the New Frontier?[41] Yoma's questions were well-put, but never anticipated by Washington. It was one thing, as Dellinger implied, to welcome overdue US concern. It was another thing to expect that concern to become an effective, working policy. To Kennedy, expressions of concern were a necessity within the New Pacific Community vision. The working policy could be put together by his successors.

With the navy eliminated from a governmental role in the islands and the Congress approving his programs, Kennedy decided that his New Frontier helmsman in Guam, Governor Daniel, was no longer needed. He called for a general election, throwing his support behind the tiny Democratic-Popular Party of Guam. Manuel F. L. Guerrero, once the underdog to Flores's well-oiled Republican machine, became the new governor. Praising Kennedy as the savior of Micronesia, Guerrero promised a generation of rapid growth and development. Kennedy's prediction of a Guamanian New Frontiersman at the helm in Agana during 1962 had become reality.[42]

The new Trust Territory administration in Saipan maintained a low key presence, making it clear that it favored full self-government for the islands. Instead of assigning mainland-born and trained officials to specific island ports, Micronesians were now picked and given full discretion in local hiring of government employees.[43] For instance, Takeo Yano of Palau in the Carolines and Prudencio Manglona of Rota in the Marianas were essentially in charge of their islands' local government, but they still answered to the Trust Territory headquarters on Saipan. Both men enjoyed this local independence; however, they remained concerned about the future. They asked Kennedy to send the special mission to the islands as soon as possible. The region's economic progress and political status, they believed, might be determined by the mission's work.

In the meantime, Yano and Manglona, as well as the Trust Territory government in general, reported a positive US-islander relationship thanks to Kennedy's Executive Order decisions and other policies. The list of new achievements was long. In all the islands, the chartering of municipalities had been strengthened. Tax exemptions on liquor for non-indigenous groups had been removed. Belabored negotiations began in June 1962 with a number of major American commercial fisheries companies for the establishment of large-scale operations in Truk and Palau. Copra and cacao co-operatives were created for expansion of trading companies activities. A slaughterhouse was built in Rota and a soap factory constructed in Palau. Bank loans were made to small private businessmen throughout the Trust Territory. And finally, the Trust Territory had, for the first time, enough money to begin airfield and road projects on all the islands. Without question, the new era of growth had begun, but its direction remained slow and unclear.[44]

Noting that America must find the best vehicle in bringing Guam and the Trust Territory into "full association" with the United States, Kennedy, on 1 May 1963, appointed Professor Anthony Solomon of the Harvard Business School to investigate development and security problems in Micronesia. The members of Solomon's mission included cabinet officials and academics. After meeting with the National Security Council (NSC), Kennedy ordered Solomon's security findings to be classified. Commander Charles Chamberlain of CINCPAC was recommended by the NSC to be attached to the Solomon mission for purposes of "fairness" and "security" in defense matters. Kennedy agreed.[45]

Solomon's work constituted the first complete analytical study of Micronesian issues undertaken by a Presidential administration. Even Solomon admitted that the mission's work uncovered a number of things that had not been considered in Pacific policy-making. First of all, he reported that Micronesia included a variety of racial mixtures, languages and cultures, representing a series of individual island communities rather than a unified society. Secondly, he reported that Micronesia lacked human and natural resources as well as adequate communications and transportation links. Indeed, no development plan considered the survival of island cultures in the rush to modernization. Thirdly, life in the islands centered around the village, the extended family or clan and its lands. The traditional system of communal land ownership, inheritance through matrilineal lines, and the selection of chiefs continued to exist side-by-side with the model democracy that America was attempting to introduce there. Facing these three lessons, as well as illiteracy and subsistence agrarian economies, Solomon predicted rough going ahead for both American-Micronesian relations and economic development.[46]

Kennedy's interest in granting what amounted to a special Pacific version of his Civil Rights Bill to the islands was not entertained by the Solomon mission. Solomon saw no relevance to the effort, the Micronesians did not yet see themselves as Americans requiring certain protections within American law. True, Guamanians had been American citizens since the Organic Act of 1950, but the Solomon mission saw Kennedy's suggestion of civil rights reform as the proverbial cart before the horse. In this case, Solomon argued, the horse should be a well-defined and guaranteed political status for the region. The cart, constitutional civil rights/civil liberties, would then follow. Solomon implied that Kennedy's rule-by-decree approach to Micronesia, no matter how well-intentioned, was not the answer in determining the region's future. On the other hand, he complimented the American government's new involvement in Micronesia. Something, he said echoing Kennedy, had to be done.[47]

Although concerned about the Kennedy administration's reaction to his findings, Solomon also worried about Micronesian opinion. Finding the pulse of Micronesian opinion on political/economic issues had been a trying process for the mission. Solomon concluded that the majority of Micronesians had little interest in mainland-inspired politics. Indeed, many islanders admitted to the mission that "political status," the "New Frontier," and "twentieth century progress" were irrelevant to their lives. Solomon wondered if this was simple apathy or a more sophisticated rejection of American influence. Whatever the answer, this type of attitude was not to the benefit of American policy. Solomon reasoned that many Micronesians saw themselves in "the American time," a situation that had replaced "the Japanese time." The earlier Spanish and German "times" were usually not remembered. Would these people welcome statehood? Would they like being symbols of America's new partnership with Pacific peoples as suggested in the New Pacific Community idea? Solomon made no predictions, but he was convinced that there was no alternative to an expanding, working American–Micronesian relationship.

> Despite a lack of serious concern for the area until quite recently, Micronesia is said to be essential to the United States for security reasons. We cannot give the area up, yet time is running out for the United States in the sense that we may soon be the only nation left administering a trust territory. The time could come, and shortly, when the pressures in the United Nations for a settlement of the status of Micronesia could become more than embarrassing.[48]

Employing the Kennedy-inspired love of analysis, Solomon offered a fine examination of Micronesian life, detailing all the variables and weighing the options. Like Kennedy, Solomon often found more questions than answers. What do the Micronesians want? Will a change in status truly eliminate the colonial-styled American relationship to the islands? Can serious commitments to Micronesian development lead to the type of political benefit and international recognition that the Kennedy administration desired? Throughout his study, Solomon implied that Micronesia might be a far-flung American outpost, but that the issues there were too complicated and frustrating to bring quick benefit to America. Solomon's "long run" offered what Kennedy really wanted to hear. "Permanent association" with the United States was Micronesia's future, Solomon declared. Growing communist tensions in the Asian/Pacific area made independence a security risk for the United States. Consequently, national self-interest dictated the future, and Micronesia would be expected to support that interest.[49]

Solomon's "permanent association" decision avoided a straightforward conclusion on statehood. He left that honor to the President.
In 1963, there were two obvious problems in defining "permanent
association." One involved the reaction of the United Nations Trusteeship Council, and the other involved the reaction of Micronesia's
small political elite. If both were pleased with the Solomon report,
the Kennedy administration would begin the process of placing
Micronesia on the path to statehood. Handsome economic aid packages (totaling to $17.5 million) would immediately accompany that
process. Significant opposition to the report was not anticipated, or,
more to the point, not contemplated.[50]

Although it made no official statement on the topic, the United
Nations supported Khrushchev's assessment of America's position
in Micronesia. On 14 December 1960 the United Nations had passed
Resolution 1514 calling for independence to all colonial peoples,
including those in the last remaining United Nations Trust, Micronesia. A Special Committee was established to implement this Resolution. Consisting of seventeen members, the Committee admitted
failure in November 1961. Hence, a new Resolution was passed by
the General Assembly. No. 1654 reiterated the declaration of the
previous year, but also praised the Kennedy administration for, at
the least, responding to Micronesian problems.

The Kennedy administration considered No. 1654, and its similar-
ly-worded version of December 1962, No. 1810, as examples of the
UN's flexibility. In short, Kennedy planned to appeal to the UN's
sense of humanitarian mission, offering the reform-minded "permanent association" as an adequate substitute for independence.
Indeed, Kennedy also considered a quick replacement of all Trust
Territory administrators with a new team. Solomon had reported
that these American administrators were sympathetic to Micronesian
independence. They had to go.[51]

Micronesia's politically active elite followed the US–UN debate
with interest. As long as "permanent association" remained ill-
defined, and statehood a distant vision, the debate promised to be
a long one. This elite consisted of a triumvirate of the traditional
clan chiefs, the educated younger bureaucracy working in the Trust
Territory government, and the tiny but powerful group of businessmen operating trading companies. Their concern continued to be
manifested in emotional arguments, not political parties. The reason
for this approach now went beyond local cultural/political traditions.
Independence equaled economic uncertainty and general insecurity.

Courting America's favor appeared to be the best policy as long as Micronesians eventually determined the nature of that policy.[52]

Without question, by late 1963, the Micronesians were contemplating their future in the same type of forward-looking terms as Kennedy employed. This did not mean that they saw themselves as part of a Washington-directed New Pacific Community or the 51st state. They welcomed Kennedy's interest, but they reserved the right to conclude this debate once and for all.[53] Naturally, there were specific items in the Solomon report that the islanders regarded above raw political consideration, such as basic health care and education. Quick agreement between the islanders and Washington over the need to assault these issues indicated that the general debate might always be conducted in a friendly, gentleman-like fashion.

Completing its work in October 1963, the Solomon mission had found the education and health systems in complete chaos. They offered a specific modernization plan based on Peace Corps and HEW advice, involving economic assistance, local technical training as well as mainland educational exchange programs, and construction. This section of the report was made public and was well-received in the islands. Kennedy promised immediate action, and especially decried Solomon's report on the spread of polio in the region. In a letter to Secretary Udall, Kennedy expressed his anger over nineteenth-century health conditions.

> I am shocked at the report on the spread of polio in the Trust Territory. It seems to me that this is inexcusable. How much would it have cost to have taken precautionary steps? Is there a difference in treatment for United States citizens in this country and the people for whom the United States is responsible in the Trust Territory? In short, I would like a complete investigation into the reason why the United States government did not meet its responsibility in this area.[54]

The Solomon mission put greater public focus on the problems of Micronesia, suggesting that this so-called minor policy issue might become a minor campaign issue during the 1964 election. Kennedy welcomed Solomon's findings, but remained convinced that all of Micronesia would soon desire statehood. If not "straightforward statehood," perhaps they would desire incorporation of the Trust Territory as a district of Hawaii and the Marianas as a separate state with Guam as its capital; a new idea Kennedy presented to the Solomon team.[55] Whatever happened, it was apparent that Kennedy

planned to begin it and focus public attention on it. In June 1963, a
delegation of Micronesian business leaders, clan spokesmen, and
bureaucrats had visited the White House and Kennedy promised to
visit Guam and the Trust Territory in return. Following the submission of the Solomon report, Kennedy announced to the cabinet
that he planned to visit the region by the end of the year or early
1964.[56] Less than one month later, he was assassinated.

Until 1961, Guam and the Trust Territory had been considered
tranquil outposts of American influence in the Pacific. Kennedy's
vision of the "pay any price, bear any burden" America did not
include tranquil outposts. Total commitment and iron determination,
he suggested in his inaugural address, would bring victory to America
in the Cold War. All Americans were invited to participate. The fact
that he included Micronesians in his definition of all Americans was
remarkable in itself.

The New Pacific Community was to be the vehicle of Micronesia's
participation in the Cold War; a vehicle that remained personally
designed by the Kennedy administration. The Micronesians were
expected to respond joyously to Washington's new generosity
towards them. Their response would be touted by American officials
across the Pacific as testimony to the death of the "ugly American."
Anti-communist commitment could indeed be wedded to democratic
reform and humanist concern.

Whether Kennedy succeeded or failed in forever influencing the
direction of Asian/Pacific politics made little difference to the
Micronesians. Of greater significance to them was Washington's new
interest in the islands and what it might mean. Kennedy did not
live to resolve the "permanent association" debate, and there is
no evidence to suggest that he planned to resolve it. Instead, his
administration offered, as it had promised, "a new beginning" for
Micronesia in the form of economic assistance and political status
studies.

Given the region's cultural and political diversity, Kennedy's statehood ambitions for Micronesia were misplaced. That fact became
obvious to Washington by the late 1960s. Statehood vision soon
translated into the Office of Micronesian Status Negotiations
(OMSN). Established during the Nixon administration, the OMSN
was housed in the Department of the Interior and it welcomed
assistance from the Defense and State Departments. Its mission was
to ask: "What do the Micronesians want?," rather than Kennedy's:
"What can the Micronesians do for us?"

The OMSN succeeded in concluding a Compact of Free Association with Micronesia. Approved by Congress and the Reagan administration in 1985, the Compact offered an unprecedented solution to "permanent association." Instead of statehood, territorial status, or independence, the Compact promised benefits from all three concepts. American security interests in the islands were guaranteed by the Compact and the Micronesians welcomed America's defense commitment to them. Meanwhile, the Americans promised non-interference in local political and economic developments within a complicated set of mutually agreed guidelines.[57]

Whether Kennedy might have approved of the Compact remains a matter of speculation. Indeed, considering its respect for specific island concerns, the Compact was more of a product of the post-Vietnam, post-Watergate era than of Kennedy's "maneuvering." Yet, as in the case of America's happy memory of Camelot, Kennedy's image remains a positive one in the islands. In the long run, this idealistic Cold Warrior combined the promise of change with an early record of achievement in Guam and the Trust Territory of the Pacific Islands. It was one of his few solid accomplishments as President, and his government's overdue interest was generally appreciated in the islands.

3 Friend or Foe? Australia and Destiny

As the Kennedy cabinet's New Pacific Community discussions stressed, America's good intentions needed proper direction. Assistance from a friendly foreign power, such as Australia, was encouraged if not demanded. But, a successful direction also depended upon the Kennedy administration's perception of Asian/Pacific developments. In the case of Micronesia, Kennedy had viewed the islands as a political/cultural whole. Statehood was their destiny, and no further conclusions were necessary. Kennedy had proven the old political dictum that perceptions of the truth in politics can be more important than truth itself. The dictum was applied to Australia as well. Kennedy's perception of Australian politics, and what America must do to influence them, did nothing for warm Australian–American relations.[1]

To Kennedy and his cabinet, Australia was a carbon copy of an American-styled democracy in the Pacific. They saw no reason against enlisting the carbon copy into a more active role in anticommunist politics throughout Asia. Moreover, they saw no reason for the Australians to reject that role. Indeed, the Kennedy team implied that Australia was already akin to the 51st state.[2] It took them over two years to discover that that was not the case. Yet, the implications of that discovery would be lost on the Kennedy White House.

In early 1961 the United States faced no important problems in its bilateral relations with Australia. Maintaining an attitude fully shared by the bulk of its electorate, the Australian government pursued a policy of open cordiality towards Washington. While remaining firmly loyal to its British Commonwealth ties, Australia had moved farther than various others among the Commonwealth countries toward viewing the United States in a special category of relationship. To John Kennedy, this happy situation always presented a clear opportunity to achieve New Frontier goals in the Pacific. But, Australia did present at least one problem. Rusk's State Department declared it too passive in the anti-communist crusade.[3] Passivity was not part of the Kennedy administration's foreign policy vocabulary. There were two reasons behind this American-placed label. The first one involved a growing Australian disgust for Washington's non-recognition policy towards the People's Republic of China (PRC). Since 1949 and the communist victory in China, the United States had insisted on "allied solidarity" in the non-recognition of the PRC. By 1961, both the Liberal and Labor Parties of Australia had grown weary of this "solidarity" and worried that Kennedy's "massive retaliation" approach might stimulate Chinese aggression in the Pacific rather than contain it. These worries were attached to the second reason behind Washington's concern over Australian Cold War "passivity," namely the desire to resolve potentially violent disputes with Indonesia over the future of nearby West New Guinea. In short, Australia sought regional peace and development. Hence, anti-China sword-rattling only delayed this goal.

Swearing full allegiance to the China non-recognition policy was not a firm prerequisite to joining Kennedy's dream of a New Pacific Community, but it would establish a certain spirit of cooperation and commitment. In any event, Kennedy's own cabinet was aware from the beginning that the odds were against them. In 1960, the Australian government had concluded a one million ton grain deal to the PRC. Trade and labor delegations were exchanged between both countries, and even Australian tourists were now welcome in China under "special conditions". One year later, an alliance of Australian businessmen were demanding economic ties with China in the interest of pulling off an Australian "economic coup" before other industrial nations shed their non-recognition policies. Meanwhile, the opposition Labor Party pressured the Australian Liberal Party government tirelessly on the issue of "innovative external affairs." An "innovative" government, they noted, embraced new policies that kept the peace and furthered economic progress. The twelve-year-old Liberal government, they concluded, was too exhausted for the 1960s and the continued Liberal bowing to Washington's China non-recognition policy symbolized the point.[4]

Times were changing for the non-recognition policy across the Pacific. In Japan, Prime Minister Hayato Ikeda called for US–China *détente* in the name of "nuclear peace." Even in the Philippines, President Carlos Garcia urged Kennedy to tone down the militant Cold War rhetoric and consider the impact of that rhetoric on an "unpredictable" nation like the PRC. To Kennedy, Ikeda's comments were within the traditional post-1945 Japanese policy against potential nuclear threats, and Garcia could be silenced via infrastructure assistance or through less expensive appeals as well.[5] Australia remained a problem because of its designed role in the New Pacific Community. Nevertheless, the slow path towards China recognition had already been made by the Australians. It would be difficult to blockade, and the Kennedy team realized that fact.[6] The administrations before and after Kennedy's might have abandoned the New Pacific Community plan because of these difficult realities, but Kennedy was challenged by them and pressed on. Australia's overtures towards China, and cautious support from other Pacific powers over the issue, were to remain frustrating developments for the Kennedy Cold Warriors. Yet, these overtures also remained slow-moving, and time, Kennedy believed, was always on America's side.

Washington saw Australia as an American-supporting champion of international issues. Canberra saw Australia as a developing nation with strong regional concerns and a rising dollar that might spread its influence into China some day. The American-Australian row that the Kennedy administration largely created itself would always be a matter of conflicting ambitions and practical politics. Australian complaints against American protectionist legislation over Australian wool products consistently amazed the Kennedy administration.[7] At a time when Kennedy depicted Asian/Pacific affairs as a deadly game of anti-communist jousting, requiring allied solidarity and vigor, the Australians preferred to talk about sweaters.

New Guinea, on the other hand, was an Australian concern that Kennedy could respect. He and his PT-boat crew had almost died near there in 1943, and the threat of Indonesian military expansionism was both real and far to the south of America's major Asian/Pacific military bases. Since 1949 Australia had wrestled with Indonesia's claim to West New Guinea, an area that the Dutch had retained from their old East Indies empire. Labeling Indonesia's claim a security risk, Canberra supported the Dutch. The resulting arguments over security versus the righteousness of decolonization promised to continue through the 1960s. Not wishing to criticize an old ally like Holland, and hoping to avoid the issue of decolonization, the Eisenhower administration had attempted to ignore the matter, considering it a minor issue outside the East–West struggle. Kennedy hoped to entertain solutions with the Australian Prime Minister.[8]

Representing one of the earliest state visits to the Kennedy administration, the Australian Prime Minister, Robert Menzies, arrived in Washington on 23 February 1961. Would the Australian leader welcome the role that Kennedy designed for his country? Although an immediate response from Menzies was not anticipated, a rejection was dismissed by Kennedy as against Australia's interests. In late February 1961, Kennedy's New Pacific Community, and Australia's precise role in it, was not yet clearly defined. When Rusk submitted his final report two months later, those roles and definitions were still absent. It was the concept that continued to intrigue the President, and he hoped that it would quickly do the same for Menzies. The Australian Prime Minister might have deserved a specific outline of the proposed organization's responsibilities, but Kennedy worried that victory in the Cold War would not wait for Australia's consideration of the "fine points." This impatience stood somewhat in contrast to Kennedy's decade-long visions for the New Frontier; however, the New Pacific Community was also expected to outlast the Kennedy administration. While his cabinet supposedly prepared the mechanics of the New Pacific Community, Kennedy planned to win an Australian commitment to economic and possible military involvements in Asia.[9]

Kennedy soon discovered that what America considered "fine points" in Australian policy constituted, in effect, the very heart of Australian external affairs. Designed to assist the President during his discussions with the Australian Prime Minister, Kennedy's lengthy State Department briefing papers only scratched the surface of Australian policy. Instead, they stressed the "image of America in Australia," and how that positive image could be exploited to achieve American policy goals in the Pacific region. Once again, no precise formula for success was noted. On the other hand, the Australian Prime Minister was expected to focus the discussion in two areas: West New Guinea and Laos–Vietnam. The State Department suggested that Kennedy offer America's "good offices" in the West New Guinea matter and urge direct Australian involvement in the Southeast Asian situation. No problems were anticipated by the State Department here. Consequently, Kennedy would have plenty of time to talk about the New Pacific Community concept.[10]

The State Department's assessment of the American image in Australia was interesting, but off the mark. Australian politics was changing. The Liberal–Country Party coalition had dominated federal politics in Australia since 1949. Its fortunes were fading in 1961 and so was the World War II-inspired image of the United States. Embracing notions of working-class solidarity as well as a vague British-type socialism, the Labor Party was on the rise. Its opinion of America reflected the popularized "ugly American" thesis in other Pacific states.

During February 1961, there were clear indications in the Australian press that the electorate was apathetic towards the continuation of the twelve-year-old Menzies government. Yet, the Labor Party suffered from an ideological split. The Party's majority tolerated a small communist wing, while a vocal minority was Catholic-led and militantly anti-communist. In any event, a 1961 general election was inevitable. The Kennedy administration expected a Menzies victory, but they did not anticipate Menzies's bowing to the new nationalist opinion in Australia. "Australian Pride" in rapid postwar economic development was now more important than American connections, and Menzies hoped to keep his coalition alive a little longer by courting such sentiments.[11]

The State Department described Menzies as "a strong friend of the United States and a fervent Anglophile."[12] That was true, but he was also an Australian politician. A leader of the Liberal Party since its inception in 1944, Menzies was a lawyer by profession and a political figure since the early 1930s. Possessing an unusually keen intellect, personal magnetism, a sharp wit and a talent for polemics, Menzies, like Kennedy, stood out in any political gathering. As a spokesman for his country's foreign policy, Menzies followed a course based on close alignment with the United Kingdom, the Commonwealth, and the United States. He even held the US Legion of Merit and was well known to American diplomats for his public praises of Franklin Roosevelt's Atlantic Charter principles of self-determination and decolonization.[13] It remained to be seen if this sixty-seven-year-old Australian considered the new young President an appropriate standard bearer of the Roosevelt legacy.

Menzies met Kennedy for a White House lunch on 23 February 1961. Discussions continued throughout the afternoon, and resumed the following morning. Kennedy's argument stressed what he considered straightforward logic. The genesis of the modern American-Australian connection, he pointed out, was in 1941. At that time, it became apparent that Commonwealth ties could not rescue Australia from Japanese aggression. America provided this rescue, demonstrating its significance to Pacific defense and development. After 1945, America as the chief force in the protection of Australian sovereignty became a primary tenet of Australian policy. That policy was soon formalized through the ANZUS Treaty between New Zealand, America, and Australia. The latter's economic growth paralleled the United States, Kennedy continued, indicating the influence of American economic thought in Australian life. In the 1960s, this economic success and the success of American–Australian relations merited new directions and a special mission. But before Kennedy could outline the basis of the New Pacific Community, Menzies indicated that it was necessary to examine lingering issues first.[14]

As the State Department predicted, Menzies regarded West New Guinea as the most important external affairs matter facing Australia. With the World War II threat of invasion still fresh in mind, Menzies worried that Indonesian–Dutch rivalry over the area might bring war to nearby Australia. Kennedy suggested that solutions were possible. Menzies was not convinced. The Australian government had always supported the position that self-determination could be worked out as long as the Dutch remained in West New Guinea and did not surrender to Indonesia's "imperial ambitions." This only suggested that one power was less "imperial" than another, avoiding the major issue at hand. That issue was Australia's fear of Indonesia itself. Turbulent politics was the norm there, and the communists always enjoyed a strong voice in governmental affairs. Menzies feared that Indonesian control of West New Guinea, or West Irian as the Indonesians called it, would cause unrest in Australian-developed East New Guinea. Hence, even if all the Pacific nations agreed to some peaceful transfer of power from Dutch New Guinea to the Indonesians, Australian security might still be threatened *vis-à-vis* East New Guinea.

Menzies stood firm on the principle of self-determination, suggesting that the problem was now, and always would be, a matter for the Dutch and their colonial subjects to work out alone. Unless Kennedy had a better solution, Menzies implied that the American government would appear in opposition to self-determination, supportive of Indonesian expansion, and apathetic over Indonesian–Australian conflicts. Kennedy's solution was based on five points, all of them playing off Menzies' long time interest in United Nations efforts. First of all, Kennedy pointed out that West New Guinea was as significant an issue in Washington as it was in Canberra. Indeed, there was some truth to the statement. An Indonesian–Dutch conflict would divert American attentions from Vietnam and Laos, forcing America to chose between an old NATO ally and a new symbol of growing Pacific power. This diversion from the larger anti-communist struggle had to be avoided. Thus, as his second point, Kennedy stressed "common interests" in Pacific peace, but noted that Indonesia demanded the "immediate removal" of the Dutch. Menzies's call for the "slow moving" self-determination process in West New Guinea would only lead to war.

Kennedy's third, fourth, and fifth points stressed America's commitment to self-determination and that it "might soon apply" to West New Guinea. In short, the latest intelligence information indicated that the Indonesian government's sword-rattling rhetoric was not being matched by mobilization efforts and war plans. This suggested that there was still time for a negotiation effort. Kennedy urged the Australian Prime Minister to avoid fatalist attitudes and accept the negotiation challenge. The challenge, he continued to outline in point-by-point fashion, would come in the form of a United Nations initiative, not a Washington solution.

In answer to a January 1961 inquiry from the Menzies government, the State Department had indicated that it supported a United Nations Trusteeship over West New Guinea. Kennedy echoed that response, suggesting that the Trust Territory of the Pacific Islands would be the model for West New Guinea. Menzies said he was expecting something different from the January 1961 policy position. On the one hand, he considered it a temporary fix that compromised self-determination and still tempted Indonesian intrigue. On the other hand, it was the only solution outside the Dutch–Indonesian reconciliation, and that did not appear on the horizon in 1961.

The Trusteeship decision raised a certain irony. Kennedy's concern over America's "ugly American" and "colonial" image in the Pacific was moving him in the direction of relinquishing the United Nations mandate over Micronesia. Yet, he favored the same-styled mandate near the heart of the area where the New Frontier was supposed to foster a new image of America. Without question, West New Guinea was a nuisance issue to Kennedy, for greater things needed to be accomplished.

We have no illusions that amelioration of this problem will resolve all questions concerning Indonesia. We are aware that Indonesia will continue to pose problems that will require our best efforts to meet. However, we believe the Indonesians, especially the large and potentially influential moderate group, will be better able to withstand the pressures of Communism and to move more rapidly to normal developments only when they no longer are distracted by this dispute.[15]

To Menzies "the most imaginative and constructive policy to come out of the Kennedy administration" thus far had been the proposal to neutralize Laos. That proposal appeared to be based on the assumption that all those who debated the future of Laos and its neighbors were reasonable men who sought peace. Menzies favored this approach over that of the "pay any price, bear any burden" rhetoric, remarking to Kennedy that it reminded him of something Roosevelt would have done. Kennedy accepted the comment as a compliment, but Menzies had meant to attach greater significance to the remark. The Laos proposal, Menzies thought, was a good one, but it also suggested pitfalls. Whereas Roosevelt might have underestimated the good faith of Stalin at Yalta, Kennedy, Menzies believed, might have underestimated the good faith of the communist bloc over Laos. The proposal called for a ceasefire guaranteed by several neutral nations in the communist versus anti-communist struggle. Success there, Kennedy hoped, would spread to nearby Vietnam. Moreover, success was contingent upon full communist participation. Menzies contended that the Kennedy administration banked too much on a happy outcome. For instance, Prince Sihanouk of Cambodia maintained a number of grievances against the Laotian government, but his participation in the proposal was essential. Kennedy could not give Menzies any assurances that Sihanouk would assist in the peacemaking. In fact, Sihanouk rejected a formal invitation to participate during the Menzies visit. Given Sihanouk's reluctance, Menzies even wondered if the neutral nations could provide "the calibre of commissioners necessary to carry out the magnitude of their tasks."

If the Laos proposal failed, Menzies predicted that America would be tempted to employ "massive retaliation" in Vietnam, or at the least, step up its involvement there. Hence, Washington would avenge its misplaced trust in communist intentions. Kennedy defended the Laos proposal, realizing that Menzies's previous allusion to a Roosevelt-Kennedy parallel might not have been a solid compliment.

> We fully realize that the success of the plan depends to a great extent on the attitude of the Communist bloc. We have reason to believe that there may possibly be a genuine desire on the part of the Soviet Union for a détente in Laos, and the plan we have proposed contains what the Communists have been saying they want for Laos.[16]

Menzies's concerns soon proved prophetic, for the proposal

resulted in an escalation of communist Pathet Lao activity, no working ceasefire, and a stronger American commitment to military,
rather than political, solutions in Vietnam. These events would, of
course, do nothing for Kennedy's idea of an American–Australian
partnership in the New Pacific Community. To Kennedy, communist
growth in the Asian/Pacific region required a stiffening of anti-communist resolve. To Menzies, communism remained an obvious evil,
but not a justification for continuous conflict or even high diplomatic
tensions. In effect, Kennedy approached the new Pacific Community
issue in a similar fashion as Micronesia. Like the Trust Territory
islanders, he was offering Australians new responsibilities and oppor-
tunities beneath an American umbrella. To add further perspective,
Kennedy depicted the New Pacific Community as a modern, 1960s
version of the traditional Commonwealth ties to Britain. Given Britain's adherence to the European Economic Community (EEC), the
Commonwealth appeared to be in a state of collapse. Menzies
planned to meet with the British government in March 1961 to
discuss its EEC decision. He expected a guarantee that London
would consult Australia if any new EEC arrangement threatened to
affect his country's exports of primary produce to Britain and
Europe. Kennedy encouraged Britain's decision and would formally
announce this support to Harold Macmillan, the British Prime Minister, during the latter's April 1961 visit to Washington.[17]

Kennedy explained to Menzies that America desired "to enter
into some kind of non-military institutional framework" with Australia and other non-communist Asian/Pacific states. The new organization would always "supplement" and not "duplicate" the work of
the United Nations and other international organizations. Kennedy
did not express Rusk's frustrations over America's lonely spearheading of anti-communism in Southeast Asia, but he offered plenty
of suggestions that challenged Australia to translate its economic/de-
mocratic success into an activist, interventionist foreign policy based
on American goals in the Cold War.

Menzies's staff received precise American policy positions on all
scheduled topics of discussion, except the New Pacific Community.
The details, Kennedy promised, were forthcoming. Meanwhile,
Menzies offered no comment beyond "the matter requires further
study." He also gave no indication that Australia's China policy
would be scrapped in favor of America's hard line. For all practical
purposes, the Kennedy–Menzies relationship in early 1961 was more
trying for the President than his cabinet had predicted. Talking

peace, Kennedy discovered, suggested more solid ground for complete agreement than anti-communist rhetoric. Nevertheless, Menzies concluded that the New Pacific Community appeared to be an effort to place Australia into some sort of "spokesman" role for American policy, and to serve as an institutional "thank you" gift in exchange for, perhaps, a large American military presence in Australia.

Despite the Australian Prime Minister's response, everything still appeared negotiable to Kennedy in 1961, and he felt that the Australians only needed time to fully accept America's position. The post-Second World War progress of American-Australian relations and the Menzies era itself might have suggested to the Kennedy administration that a special lure was not necessary. But this realization would also imply that America welcomed and respected Australia's tactically different approach to anti-communism in the Pacific region.[18] In 1961, this type of response from the Kennedy administration was unlikely, for it would negate the concepts of solidarity and commitment that were part of the New Frontier mission for the Pacific.

Time proved to be against New Frontier idealism. As the Bay of Pigs and Berlin Wall episodes indicated, Cold War tensions were increasing without any Cold War victory in sight. Time was an enemy to Menzies as well. In December 1961, the Menzies government lost its comfortable majority in Parliament, emerging from a general election with a paper-thin majority of one in the 124-seat House of Representatives and retaining only 30 of 60 seats in the less crucial Senate. Although the Menzies government continued in office on the strength of its slender majority in the House, its tenure was suspected to be short by the Kennedy administration. In early 1962, Washington now expected to be dealing with a Labor government by the end of the year. Foreign policy had played little part in the Australian election of 1961. The government's losses were attributed to dissatisfactions over deflationary measures. Enacted in late 1960, these measures were supposed to curb what Menzies considered to be an increasingly unhealthy boom. Instead, this approach brought about a sharp increase in unemployment, fueling the political charge that the aging Menzies government had lost touch with the common man.[19]

In February 1961, Menzies's unexpected and unwanted replies to American policy goals had surprised both the State Department and the White House. For the next several months, Rusk and Kennedy did their best to ignore American–Australian matters. But during November 1961, George Ball, the new Under Secretary of State, announced that the New Pacific Community was still a worthy project. First of all, he asked for and received several studies from the American Embassy in Canberra on "the nature of the Australian character" as part of an effort to decide on whether Menzies had represented a legitimate protest to American policy or if he symbolized an independent, frontier-like spirit. As interested in symbols as most New Frontiersmen, Ball, a longtime Democratic Party activist and foreign policy theorist, concluded that the American and Australian approach to politics continued to enjoy more similarities than differences. Consequently, he suggested to an agreeable Kennedy that his administration adjust to the changing Australian political scene as it had done elsewhere in 1961. The adjustment would come in four areas of stress, (1) mediation of the Dutch–Indonesian dispute over New Guinea, (2) a "significant" military base "of any size" in Australia, (3) Australian assistance of "any kind" in Southeast Asia, and (4) new discussions on the New Pacific Community.[20] By March 1962, America's great plans for Australia in the Pacific had been restricted to a simple working relationship with a promise for the future, the New Pacific Community.

American policy adjustments were necessary, the Kennedy administration had reasoned, to fit the struggling Menzies government and appeal to Menzies's probable successors in the Labor party. A Labor victory at the polls, Ball wrote to Kennedy, would bring to power a government which, although not necessarily antithetical to American interests, "could be expected to retreat somewhat from the open cooperation of the present Government and to espouse divergent policies in defense matters."[21] The ease with which American entrepreneurs invested and did business in Australia had become a primary issue in Labor party politics. Championed by Gough Whitlam, the Deputy Leader of the Opposition, the fight against undue American influence on the economy tempered the Menzies government's pro forma public statements of praise for the United States. According to Kennedy, once again, the promise of a "new partnership" in the Pacific appeared to be the appropriate vehicle to defuse any anti-American sentiment that the investments/business issue might stimulate.[22] The goal remained to win significant support for United States policy in Southeast Asia. Indeed, the Laos neutralization scheme was not working, and Kennedy recognized that Menzies's criticism of it might have been correct. He even admitted to Menzies in 1962 that he had overestimated the communist cry for peace. Feeling that his efforts to maintain a truce in Laos had been exploited by the communists, Kennedy told Menzies that America "and Australia" must not permit a security gap in Southeast Asia. The future of a non-communist Southeast Asia now appeared, as Menzies predicted, to be centered in South Vietnam behind the shaky Diem regime. Australia reassured the Thais at a May 1962 ANZUS meeting that SEATO members were prepared to honor their anti-communist commitments effectively and that Southeast Asia could expect further American–Australian action in the future. These expectations were given further credence when, at the end of this meeting, Australia volunteered thirty military instructors to South Vietnam. Moreover, by the time of Kennedy's November 1963 assassination, Australia volunteered communications equipment, barbed wire, and other materials for village defense.[23] All of this lacked the dramatic commitment that Kennedy sought, but it was accomplished during a changing political climate in Australia and when the EEC issue still dominated most matters related to Australian economic affairs, including foreign aid.

Kennedy had hoped to expand the Australian approach to Southeast Asia by appealing to anti-communist sentiments and the principles incorporated within the New Pacific Community idea. America's interest in what the Kennedy administration had come to consider "Australia's West New Guinea issue" offered a precedent for Canberra to embrace Washington's issue of Southeast Asia. By June 1962, Australia's position on West New Guinea had shifted from extreme opposition towards Indonesia's plans to one of reluctant acquiescence in having Indonesia for a neighbor in Papua New Guinea. America's interest in solving the issue via international channels remained unchanged, and in February 1962, the President's brother, Attorney General Robert Kennedy, acted as the American emissary in the dispute.[24] Such personal involvements symbolized America's interest in all Pacific matters important to Australia. Hence, the President presented his case for Australian military/economic involvement in South Vietnam during 1962 with the same type of symbolic arguments used throughout the previous year.

It remained disturbing for the Kennedy administration to have its New Frontier vision of the Pacific skirted by its major ally in the region. The State Department sent Kennedy a flurry of memoranda on the subject, assuring him that Australia would eventually become deeply involved in Southeast Asia.[25] In the meantime, the Kennedy administration prepared to open its new military base in Australia. As the only solid point of agreement in 1962, a small, isolated American–Australian military base in northwest Australia suddenly held great significance to the future of American–Australian relations.

Far from the vision of 1961, the base was to be a naval communications station in Western Australia at North West Cape. The Western Australian government volunteered its assistance in initial survey activities, and Menzies urged the entire Parliament to welcome the endeavor. The purpose of the station, which included a complex antenna system, high powered transmitting and receiving equipment, and administrative and supporting facilities, was to provide radio communications for American and Australian ships over a wide area of the Indian Ocean and the Western Pacific. The movements of potentially hostile foreign vessels were to be surveyed as well. The power supply would be provided by conventional-type diesel motors scattered over a 28 square mile area. Promising to pay all construction costs, the American government concluded contracts with Australian construction firms and hired over 1,000 Australian laborers. The base was expected to quarter 450 American navy personnel, a small Australian detachment, plus dependents.[26]

Construction began in 1963 and was completed two years later. Yet, even before any work was begun, the base project met some opposition. The *Sydney Mirror* charged that the real mission of the base was to house nuclear weapons as a reserve to America's Southeast Asia adventures. Calling for immediate investigations, other newspapers made similar charges, and the Labor Party, which advocated a nuclear free Pacific, supported these press editorials. The nuclear stockpile issue had no basis in fact, but Kennedy's appointment of a new Ambassador during the middle of the debate suggested to believers of this secret weapons tale that a Kennedy stalwart had been sent to keep matters quiet.[27] Ambassador William Battle, son of John Battle, the former Governor of Virginia, had first met Kennedy when they were both in command of PT boats at Tulagi in the Solomon Islands. A wealthy lawyer, Battle was known for his serious manner and passionate loyalty to Kennedy. His "no comments" to the press on United States defense interests in Australia stimulated further curiosities.[28]

By October 1963, the Menzies government, facing another election, began to echo the Labor party and the press on all nuclear issues. During that month, the ANZUS Council urged the United

States to study the possibility of creating a nuclear free zone for the Pacific region. The United Nations was already considering a nuclear free zone resolution for Latin America. If it succeeded, Australia expected Washington's support for a Pacific version. Kennedy affirmed America's opposition to nuclear free zones anywhere in the world, declaring them "impractical." He admitted a sympathy for the case; however, he asked that this sympathy never be discussed with the press. Using the issue as a transition to the New Pacific Community, the Australian government pointed out that the nuclear matter indicated certain differences of opinion between the two countries. Since the New Pacific Community appeared to be a vehicle for Australia to voice American policy priorities, Canberra's participation would be inappropriate. It was Australia's final word.[29]

Until late 1963, the Australian government had been most diplomatic in dealing with Kennedy on the issue of democratic solidarity in the Pacific. Canberra's blunt refusal had been two years in coming, reflecting both the Menzies government's latest political struggles and Kennedy's approach to policy. During 1962 Kennedy's confrontational approach to the cold war had, of course, helped lead the world to near nuclear disaster over the future of Soviet influence in the Western Hemisphere and Cuba's missile-based defense. His rhetoric on behalf of peace and freedom in the Third World continued to have little impact on the progress of events there. Yet, outside of crisis management, he was slow in making policy, suggesting to many that he doubted his own rhetoric of commitment and confrontation. The Menzies government had had this impression from the beginning, and Kennedy's expressed sympathies towards Australian concerns, such as the nuclear free Pacific, seemed to confirm it.[30] Nevertheless, Kennedy persisted with the New Pacific Community, as if discarding it would mean abandoning the early dreams of the New Frontier. In the long run, this was the only justification for keeping the idea alive, for the New Pacific Community symbolized another nation's conforming to American policy, not solidarity with it.

Kennedy finally learned the difference between conformity and solidarity just days before his assassination. Diem was also assassinated in a coup encouraged by the American President himself. The South Vietnamese leader had refused to adjust his country's policies to include Washington's vision of reform and political harmony. The coup disturbed Kennedy, however. Diem's death had not been part of the vision. Indeed, Kennedy's Australian policy was generally regarded in the administration and the State Department as a footnote to larger concerns, such as Southeast Asia and the hard line against mainland China. Given that situation, an early New Frontier idea like the New Pacific Community did not warrant close scrutiny or revision as the months went by. Moreover, the Australian–American partnership in the New Pacific Community came to represent a certain innocence, in February 1961, when the future appeared bright and uncomplicated. Australia was expected to accept its new role with enthusiasm. Its reluctance to do so, and eventual refusal, was difficult for the administration to accept. Personality even had a role in the tale. From boyhood, John Kennedy and his three brothers had been taught never to shrink in the face of adversity. Consequently, a "no" from a friend, Australia, could not be tolerated.[31] Kennedy's late discovery that Australia could say "no" and still remain a friend to American policy must have been an amazing, hard-in-coming revelation for him.

The revelation did not imply a significant shift in American-Australian relations or even Southeast Asia policy. The New Pacific Community remained an important idea in an administration that enjoyed discussing ideas, options, and goals. Without question, the Kennedy cabinet was convinced of America's ability to solve Asian/Pacific issues whether Australia accepted Washington's path to success or not. With a certain self-righteousness, the Kennedy team considered the basic framework of the Australian-headquartered New Pacific Community a fine legacy to leave the next Presidential administration. Instead, they left a legacy of deepening involvement in Southeast Asia and tried the patience of a proud ally, Australia.

4 New Frontier v. Guided Democracy: Kennedy, Sukarno, and Indonesia

Reflecting on his days in the Kennedy administration, Arthur Schlesinger, Jr wrote in *A Thousand Days: John F. Kennedy in the White House* that "Indonesia and Vietnam presented Kennedy with problems to which there were no clear or easy answers and which harassed him throughout his administration."[1] Indeed, in terms of official visits, negotiations, length of cabinet discussions, and stacks of policy papers, Indonesia occupied more of the young President's time than even Vietnam.[2] Although the issues and circumstances of Indonesia and Vietnam differed, the Kennedy administration attempted to place Southeast Asian affairs within general and hopeful policy goals for the entire Pacific region. At first glance, it was obvious that Indonesia was a stumbling-block to the Kennedy administration's plans for American–Pacific nation harmony in the New Pacific Community. Many Indonesians supported the communists, while others supported a unique version of democracy. Some, regardless of their political stripes, welcomed an expansionist foreign policy that demonstrated Indonesian power in Pacific affairs as well as offered guidance to Southeast Asia in the politics of anti-Western imperialism.

Indonesia's post-colonial pride and prestige were manifested in the policies of President Achmed Sukarno. Could the White House truly end the era of "ugly Americanism" and win the favor of this man? If the Kennedy team achieved victory here, Sukarno's influence, working with America, might keep the peace and stimulate development throughout the Asian/Pacific region. The New Pacific Community would be a working reality.

American-Indonesian relations offered yet another thrilling challenge to the Kennedy administration. It also promised tough decisions and the trying times of crisis management. Without question, President Sukarno presented certain difficulties to American policymakers before the creation of the New Frontier. Kennedy would heighten the drama, stimulating a US–Indonesian struggle for those much discussed "hearts and minds" of Asian/Pacific peoples.

51

By 1961, President Sukarno was already a living legend in Indonesia. In fact, given the Indonesian leader's flamboyant personality, the State Department believed that even Sukarno saw himself as a legend.[3] Having fought both the Japanese occupation during World War II and the post-war restoration of Dutch colonial rule, Sukarno had been a leader of Indonesian nationalism since 1927. Declaring Indonesia's independence in front of his own house in August 1945, Sukarno announced that the Dutch era of 300 years was over and a new era based on nationalism, humanism, democracy, social justice, and Allah, "The Five Principles," was about to begin. The declaration assured him the position of First President, as well as encouraged violent opposition from Indonesian communists. Also enjoying a strong anti-Japanese, anti-Dutch reputation, the communists had staged an impressive revolt against the Dutch as early as 1926 and had been an especially effective menace to the Japanese occupation authorities.

By 1950, Sukarno's "Five Principles" supporters had defeated the Dutch, reducing the latter's old Pacific empire to West Irian in New Guinea. The Netherlands government explained that it preferred to maintain a foothold there, simply because western New Guinea's "primitive" inhabitants did not oppose Dutch rule. More to the point, the Dutch dreamed of Sukarno's collapse and their possible return to glory. Meanwhile, Sukarno's militant communist opponents met a similar fate to the Dutch; however, political factions within the ranks of Sukarno's anti-Dutch, anti-communist forces made it difficult for the new Indonesian President to hold elections and create a working Parliament.

Taking the Parliament's functional liabilities into account, still fearing the attraction to communism for many of his countrymen, and protesting the post-Dutch liberation constitution that granted strong policy-making powers to the Parliament's Prime Minister, Sukarno assumed full governmental authority in 1957. "I can't and I won't ride a three-legged horse," he told the press, referring to Indonesia's three major political parties. The missing fourth leg remained the communists. Largely in an effort to check and control communist growth, as well as establish a certain harmony beneath his regime, Sukarno welcomed communists in his cabinet. This approach confused and shocked many Indonesians, leading to a 1958 rebellion in Sumatra.

By 1959, Sukarno favored the return to a 1945 constitution which had guaranteed strong Presidential powers during the crusade against the Dutch. The Parliament refused this formal shift in power, and by 1960 Sukarno had suspended party politics in Indonesia, including the activities of anti-Sukarno newspapers. This did not mean, the President pointed out, the death of democracy. It only meant the end of the Western-styled approach to democracy. Liberal democratic thought had no place in Indonesia, he stressed. To Sukarno, a new Asian nation required strong leadership in order to: (1) survive and develop in a world divided over the American-Soviet Cold War, and (2) maintain Indonesian integrity in the face of this bipolar world. For instance, adopting America's two party system, he concluded, would lead to violent disaster in Indonesia. "Guided Democracy" was the answer, and it was rooted in Indonesian culture and history specifically and in Asian solidarity and identity generally.[4]

Sukarno was not the first Third World leader to suggest that nationalism was more important to post-colonial development than choosing sides in the Cold War. Moreover, few Indonesians debated whether or not Sukarno's approach was original. The focus of their concern remained the nature of Guided Democracy itself. According to Sukarno, the concept lived on in the ancient village practices of *musjawarah* and *mjfakat* (mutual discussion and mutual agreement). During village discussions, everyone's voice was welcome, he pointed out. Agreements, acceptable to the whole village, were made without voting. The village elder, or leader, would resolve disagreements. Likening himself to a village spokesman, Sukarno often noted that "democracy was a means, not an end." Consequently, his Provisional People's Congress, cabinet, and other government mechanisms had no voting power. Urging cooperation and discussion between all factions of Indonesian political life, including communists, Sukarno's pleas for unity depended on support from the military and from a receptive public opinion that found him most appealing.[5]

While Sukarno owed much of his success to charisma, another charismatic political leader, John F. Kennedy, considered Sukarno's government synonymous to "capricious personal despotism."[6] Although Kennedy's presidential campaign had promised "new beginnings" and peace, his publicly-stated support for "massive retaliation" against communist threats, criticism of the Eisenhower administration's alleged defense gaps, and his Truman Doctrine-inspired rhetoric of "total commitment" suggested a militant continu-ation of the Cold War to Sukarno and others. If this approach truly became American policy, non-aligned states, and/or Third World nations who courted Soviet assistance, would become communist collaborators in the eyes of United States policy-makers. Indeed, to an extent, Washington already shared such sentiments,[7]

Having witnessed the growth of non-alignment causes in the Third World, the Eisenhower administration had often expressed its displeasure over it. For example, this displeasure was manifested in the 1958 CIA-plotted effort to overthrow Sukarno. The effort failed, but the Indonesian leader believed that the United States would have succeeded had it championed a clear, coordinated policy to quickly destroy those governments which failed to embrace its Cold War position. Viewing Sukarno as the most powerful spokesman for Third World complaints against the Cold War, the Eisenhower administration had elevated the Indonesian leader above the other non-alignment crusaders in India, Egypt, and elsewhere. Much of the Eisenhower administration's conclusion was based on Sukarno's angry rhetoric and his announcement in 1953 that Indonesia would never, under any circumstances, "play favorites" in the Cold War. Between 1953 and 1958, Secretary of State Dulles queried the Indonesian government on its anti-colonial and neutralist policies, hoping to find a break in Sukarno's hard line commitment to non-alignment. Any breaking away from that position, Dulles promised Sukarno, would lead to generous economic assistance from Washington. Sukarno, in turn, denounced Dulles's hopes as symbolic of American economic imperialism.

During this five year period of deadlock, the Eisenhower administration slowly realized that American influence over Third World opinion was limited. Destroying the source of this hostile opinion soon became the final policy option for Dulles and the President. Like Sukarno, Dulles began to see certain policies in a symbolic light. In spite of his impoverished, forever struggling nation, Sukarno's stature continued to grow as a defender of Third World nationalism. To Dulles, this development symbolized the viability of the "domino theory." Sukarno's non-alignment included anti-American sloganism as well as the toleration of internal Communist Party growth. According to Dulles, this was the political equivalent of collaboration with the Soviet position in the Cold War. Sukarno's leadership could stimulate the collapse of neighboring non-communist governments, and the beneficiary of this type of "domino" effect would always be the Soviet Union. Moreover, if Sukarno died or was displaced, his successors, the Eisenhower administration first theorized, would most likely be Indonesian communists. Hence, Washington remained deeply concerned about the progress of

US–Indonesian relations, but, outside of economic aid offers, had no idea how to improve that relationship.

Convinced that the Indonesian military viewed non-alignment from Washington's perspective, Dulles persuaded President Eisenhower to support a violent coup against Sukarno. Although offered guidance by the CIA, this short-lived, Sumatra-based coup resulted in the deaths or capture of its military adherents. The episode forced the Eisenhower administration into an active campaign to deny Sukarno's charge that the US was involved in this messy matter. American policy now stressed a Third World public relations effort to expose Sukarno's megalomania and "false charges," for fermenting coups was not in the best tradition of American democracy.

American–Indonesian relations remained eerily quiet during the latter months of the Eisenhower administration. The Eisenhower team had played its hand, and it remained in the realm of failed efforts to thwart Sukarno's alleged collaboration with Soviet expansionism. The incoming Kennedy administration saw international relations, and Indonesia's role, in a more complicated light. Largely because of Kennedy's appreciation of the Third World's significance in the Cold War, plus an apparent desire to challenge popular political figures like Sukarno, the new administration preferred to entertain more successful policy options. Throughout 1960 and January 1961, candidate and President-elect Kennedy appeared to be "guaranteeing," according to Sukarno, an American-led victory in the Cold War. This worried the Indonesian leader, and he successfully petitioned Washington for an early meeting with the new President to discuss Kennedy's vision of Pacific development, Indonesia's place in it, and the future of Holland's West Irian. Considering the nearby Dutch colony a security threat to Indonesia, Sukarno offered his own threat of invasion within his New Year's 1961 message to Holland. He implied in that message that Holland's position in NATO made little difference to him. If he had to fight Holland, America, or the "world," he promised a bloody battle.[8]

By spring 1961, Sukarno learned that there was a difference between Kennedy's vague, publicly-stated goals for "New Frontier" diplomacy and the President's private ambitions for Pacific peace and development. Kennedy welcomed Sukarno's request to visit the White House during the spring of 1961; however, he wanted a clear and workable Indonesia policy before that meeting. The American President's perception of Sukarno was not a flattering one. He considered the Indonesian leader a vain man of limited intellectual prowess. This vanity, Kennedy told Secretary of State Dean Rusk in early 1961, kept Indonesia a "backwater," for Sukarno cared more about crowd-pleasing, sword-rattling gestures against the Dutch in West Irian than about modernizing his own country. To Kennedy, Sukarno posed obvious problems to American policy in the 1960s. Given its valuable resources of tin, oil, and rubber, Indonesia, Kennedy told his cabinet, "is the most significant nation in Southeast Asia." Sukarno's courting of the Soviet Union for military assistance in a probable war against Dutch West Irian also disturbed Kennedy. The Indonesian people and army needed an American guarantee of protection against communism, Kennedy concluded.[9] Symbolizing this guarantee, and American role in preventing the Indonesian-Dutch West Irian war could also become "the key" to successful American influence on Indonesian politics for the rest of the decade.

To Kennedy, the above conclusions were simple, straightforward policy concerns. Putting them in the framework of New Frontier ambition made matters more complicated. For all practical purposes, the Kennedy cabinet's endeavor to draw distinctions between immediate policy concerns for Indonesia and decade-long New Frontier policy goals stimulated interesting cabinet discussions and little else. But distinctions or not, the thrust of Kennedy's policy was based on fear of communist growth in Indonesia and Guided Democracy's toleration of it. New Frontier rhetoric provided two long-term policy propositions in the Kennedy cabinet's Indonesia discussions of early 1961. First, there was the age-old problem of the place of morality in foreign affairs. As they demonstrated in Micronesian matters, Kennedy and his cabinet agreed that the Third World's development problems required a sympathetic American response. Staunch anti-communism as a prerequisite for American support only encouraged Sukarno and Southeast Asian nationalism, a State Department "Indonesia Plan of Action" memo pointed out to Kennedy. The New Frontier must encourage Indonesian–American cooperation, if American-styled democracy is to displace the growing popularity of communism in the villages of Southeast Asia, the State Department noted.[10]

American support for democratic and economic reforms from the village level on up might also displace the "ugly American" image of the colonial-like nation, obsessed with crushing communism and blind to the special needs of the Third World. Between late January and March 1961, *The Ugly American* was often used as a reference point in cabinet discussions that stressed the winning of the Indonesian people away from communism and totalitarianism in general. Although the President doubted its effectiveness in 1961, the Peace Corps idea slowly began to symbolize the moral promise of the New Frontier, i.e., the suggestion that the interaction of highly educated, professionally dedicated Americans and Third World peoples would lead to an American–Third World partnership. Burying the "Ugly American" image forever, this partnership would also thwart communist growth within at least a decade's time.

To Kennedy, the Peace Corps approach eventually offered a certain moral focus to American policy and, by late 1962, he wanted Indonesia to have Southeast Asia's largest contingent of volunteers.[11] Meanwhile, he wondered how Indonesia might be brought into the New Pacific Community. Would Sukarno view it as a sounding board for United States policy? The whole approach of a friendly America, listening and responding to Southeast Asian development issues, might easily backfire. If the New Pacific Community was seen by the Indonesians and others as an effort to better coordinate political or military attacks against communists and Sukarno, American policy would fail. Nevertheless, Rusk found the risk intriguing. If the New Pacific Community became policy, America would have to persuade the Southeast Asian and Pacific nations that the new organization represented a shift in United States policy based more on cooperation and concern than anti-communism. Kennedy thought it could be done, promising an exciting future as well as a clever means of isolating Sukarno and influencing Indonesian events. This situation could result whether or not Indonesia joined the New Pacific Community.[12]

Kennedy did not meet Sukarno with the clear, coordinated policy that he had desired. It troubled him. He planned to let the progress of the meeting determine the future of items such as the Peace Corps initiative to Indonesia or the New Pacific Community. Rusk reminded him that the State Department had no longstanding policy *vis-à-vis* New Guinea issues, but it had one for Holland. Rusk's comments suggested to Kennedy that America would be forced to back its NATO ally in war over West Irian. Personally, he believed that the Dutch would not fight Sukarno, for they had refused to take military action over the former Dutch colonies of Java and Sumatra. Mediating the dispute remained the best policy, he still believed. But something more was needed. The Indonesian leader "can be maneuvered," Kennedy said before meeting Sukarno, for the benefit of American policy and Pacific peace.[13]

Upon meeting the Indonesian leader, Kennedy was convinced that this original opinion of him was sound. Always vain and sometimes incoherent, Sukarno was adamant in demanding an end to Dutch colonialism, implying to Kennedy that the situation might result in America and Holland versus the Soviet Union and Indonesia over West Irian. Meanwhile, Sukarno explained Guided Democracy to Kennedy, stressing the point that Western democracies had failed to understand Southeast Asian cultures and ambitions. In turn, Kennedy explained the New Frontier, stressing the point of partnership. America, he said, now denounced foreign intrigue based on raw anti-communist goals. Although he did not offer any specifics, he suggested that America, Indonesia, and the Southeast Asian nations could strengthen democratic principles in the Pacific region by fulfilling the desire of its residents for political freedom and economic improvement. Such a partnership would stunt communist growth, he predicted.[14] Keeping the peace over the New Guinea matter would be the first step towards achieving this happy future.

Kennedy's approach remained consistent with his public "new beginnings" rhetoric, but he never found "the right key." Avoiding the specifics of his proposed American–Indonesia partnership indicated the critical problem with the New Frontier for the Pacific. It continued to suffer from a number of often conflicting ambitions, i.e., national self-interest, militant anti-communism, the desire for a distinctly Kennedy policy, the Peace Corps moral focus, the New Pacific Community promise, maneuvering foreign governments, humanist concern, and denouncing "ugly" Americanism. To Sukarno, the clearest distinction between Kennedy's militant rhetoric on Cold War-related matters and his private approach was an apparently sincere commitment to Pacific peace and development. Writing to Kennedy in December 1961, Sukarno recalled the spring meeting and he complimented Kennedy on his sincerity. This did not mean that Sukarno welcomed the New Frontier.[15] The West Irian problem lingered into 1962. To both Sukarno and Kennedy, its resolution offered the possibility of warmer American–Indonesian relations.

Further complicating the new era of warmth remained the issue of Soviet–Indonesian relations. The State Department saw the Soviet Union as a confusing one, but Kennedy demanded a clear assessment of the issue. Throughout the Kennedy administration, the State Department provided mounds of data to the White House; however, this rarely guaranteed an end to confusion. Was Moscow more effective in wooing Sukarno than Washington? The dollar figures suggested an affirmative answer.

According to the State Department's Bureau of Intelligence and Research, from 1954 to 1962, the Soviets had extended economic credits and grants totalling $4.9 billion to countries outside the communist bloc. This figure did not include military credits and grants. Five countries had received almost three-quarters of the total amount, namely India $950 million, Egypt $671 million, Indonesia $641 million, Afghanistan $515 million, and Cuba $437 million. The remainder was distributed amount 24 other countries, but by mid-1962 only Indonesia had claimed the full amount. India, for instance, had drawn only $224 million.[16]

In November 1962, the State Department concluded that only certain "presumptions" could be made about the significance of Soviet economic aid to Indonesia.

> The present power situation in Indonesia certainly has advantages for them [Soviets], not least in the flow of friendly words from President Sukarno. By providing their aid, economic as well as military, the Soviet leaders presumably hope to forestall a major crackdown on the Indonesian Communists.[17]

In short, the Soviets were as concerned over Sukarno's ambitions as the Americans, and they wondered if his oratory also equalled policy positions.[18] The Soviets had already tried to buy the protection of their communist allies in non-aligned Egypt during the mid-1950s. Their efforts failed, hence economic favors alone would not assure success in Indonesia as well.

Khrushchev had visited Indonesia during February 1960. In Djakarta, he suggested that Soviet economic generosity would soon include armaments.

> The Soviet Union has always lent and intends to continue lending friendly and disinterested assistance and support to all countries in their struggle for freedom and independence and in their efforts to overcome their age-long economic backwardness.[19]

In practical terms, Khrushchev's friendly comments led to the offering of a Soviet cruiser to the Indonesian navy and a formal invitation to discuss more sweeping and dramatic arms arrangements. Attacked by Western governments and the press for escalating the armaments race in Southeast Asia, Khrushchev replied that missiles and long-range bombers had made naval cruisers obsolete in a full

scale war. The cruiser was a "simple" Soviet gift. The West, Khrushchev said, exaggerated its significance. But, it was the Soviet Premier's invitation to arms arrangements that disturbed Washington.[20]
In January 1961, General Abdul H. Nasution, the Indonesian Minister for National Security and Chief of Staff of the Army, led a
delegation to Moscow and concluded an agreement for the purchase
of arms for all services of the Indonesian Armed Forces.

The State Department estimated the Nasution deal to be worth
$400 million. Subsequent agreements in 1961, 1962, and early 1963
increased the size of the program to nearly $1 billion. The only
comparable Soviet arms agreement was with Cuba, and that agreement was broken following the October 1962 missile crisis. In contrast to Cuba or India, the Sukarno regime was more interested in
the training of military personnel than in missiles, MIG-21 fighters,
or other exotic hardware. Sukarno promised to modernize his military, well-experienced in the area of guerrilla warfare, with the latest
technology and continental-styled strategies. This wedding of Soviet
military techniques to the guerrilla forces who triumphed over the
Japanese and Dutch was meant to impress and worry neighboring
governments. It did. Sukarno touted his military as a new symbol of
Southeast Asian power.[21]

What did Indonesia plan to do with this symbol? Was Indonesia
an aspiring Great Power? The state Department advocated a wait-
and-see approach to these questions, but also praised President Kennedy for his efforts to answer them for Indonesia. In the long run,
there were few indications coming out of Djakarta that suggested
Sukarno's military relations with the Soviets created an immediate
crisis for the United States. Nevertheless, Kennedy closely watched
those indications. For instance, on October 5 1962, Adam Malik,
the Indonesian Ambassador to the Soviet Union, remarked that the
present strength of the Indonesian navy alone had altered the balance
of power in Southeast Asia. Admittedly, Malik made his remarks
on Indonesia's Armed Forces Day and with a certain patriotic flair.
But, the State Department worried about the location of the speech
and the Soviet reaction to it. Malik delivered his address on Radio
Moscow. Tass as well as PIA, the Indonesian news agency, reported
that the Kremlin's "top brass" had accompanied Malik to the radio
studios. Both news agencies concluded that Moscow's excitement
over the Malik speech was in recognition of Indonesia's new status
as the "leading military power" in Southeast Asia.[22]

The Australian government complained nervously that the Indonesians celebrated Malik's speech by sending twenty submarines on maneuvers dangerously close to Australian waters. The incident troubled Menzies, for the Australian navy had no submarines at all. Meanwhile, the British overlords of Hong Kong colony publicly proclaimed that Indonesia's sword-rattling was somehow harming their home's economic boom. Suspicions of Indonesia's intentions were translating into cautious and limited investments by first-time investors in Hong Kong. The colonial government theorized that Sukarno sought the unassailed leadership of the African–Asian non-aligned nations. Perhaps an American recognition of that leadership, they hinted, might calm him.[23]

The Philippines government criticized both Canberra and Hong Kong for their alarmist concerns, noting that they gave Sukarno too much credit as a national leader. To the Philippines, Sukarno was "90% bluff and 10% substance." Perhaps the Filipinos inflated the percentages for their argument, but they raised a valid point. Indonesia's combination of Soviet-inspired military strength, economic weakness, and political ruthlessness suggested an image of collapse to many Indonesia watchers, including Filipinos. Certainly, Sukarno maintained his position based on personality. The Indonesian leader could not expect to continue in power based on fading images of anti-Japanese anti-Dutch heroism. The Manila government predicted that Sukarno would fall before he attempted to influence events outside of Indonesia. The resulting chaos, they said, should be Australia and Hong Kong's real worry.[24]

Manila's view of the situation reflected its own struggle with economic development and search for international respect. It also closely resembled Kennedy's policy of heading off disaster in Indonesia. But the Philippines was not a mouthpiece for American interests, even though Nazir Pamuntjak, the Indonesian Ambassador to the Philippines, proclaimed that it was.[25] In December 1962, Pamuntjak accused the Manila government of spearheading an American-instigated anti-Indonesian movement in the Pacific. Until now, he said during a radio interview, President Sukarno had viewed the Philippines as a friendly nation. But evidence had mounted concerning "a conspiracy of Asian nations" against him. Pamuntjak never named the conspirators outside of the Philippines. He simply noted his fear that Washington was behind it all. The matter, he insisted, called for a strengthening of the Indonesian military in the name of security; however, he was quick to add that Indonesia had no quarrel with the "people" of the Philippines. The tension could be easily relieved, he declared, if the Philippines government apologized for its critical comments against President Sukarno and stopped "circulating false reports" about Indonesian militarism. It was the Philippines, not Indonesia, that was disturbing economic growth in Hong Kong and elsewhere.[26]

The Philippines government dismissed Pamuntjak as a raving propagandist, but the State Department added his comments to its list of concerns. What the Kennedy administration found unsettling was that Pamuntjak's cockiness appeared to be linked to an effort to build an Indonesian version of the New Pacific Community.[27] Throughout 1961, the American Embassy in Indonesia attempted to follow and pinpoint the activities of Professor M. Yamin, Deputy First Minister in charge of Information and Chairman of the National Planning Council. Yamin, a close friend of Pamuntjak, spent much of 1961 and 1962 working on a proposal to create the Federation of Malayan States. The Federation, headquartered in Indonesia, would include the Philippines, Malaya, and the "Austronesian peoples on the islands in the Pacific Ocean and Madagascar who are still being suppressed."[28]. Consequently, Pamutjak's radio ravings were viewed by the State Department as Indonesia's way of laying a groundwork for the "new century" of Indonesian greatness. The "new century" would require Manila's submission to Indonesian power in the Federation of Malayan States.

There is no evidence to suggest that Yamin won his idea for a new Pacific organization from the Kennedy administration or even vice versa. Throughout his career as a nationalist politician, historian, poet, and writer, Professor Yamin had advocated an Indonesian imperialism that laid claim to all territories inhabited by Malay-speaking peoples. At the end of the Japanese occupation, he asserted that Malaya, Borneo, and Timor should become part of an independent Indonesia. As late as 17 February 1960, in addressing the All-Indonesian Youth Congress in Bandung, Yamin noted that his position remained unchanged.[29] One year later, he advocated war against the Portuguese in Timor, the British in North Borneo, and the Dutch in West Irian. Victory was expected in all cases, demonstrating Indonesia's Great Power status and leading role in determining the future of the Asian/Pacific region. The Federation, as loosely defined in mission and scope as the New Pacific Community, was that future.

Yamin died in early October 1962. Within a few weeks, Sukarno denounced him as the major force behind Indonesian militarism.

Yamin, he complained, had polluted Indonesia's peaceful mission in world affairs.[30] Thus, Sukarno distanced himself from the ultra-nationalist elements of his government, presenting an unusually moderate side to Indonesian politics. The Federation idea died with Yamin, while Sukarno found moderation an attractive means to hold power. To Kennedy, Sukarno's attacks on his dead comrade's ambitions was a good sign. If sword-rattling was only meant to appease nationalist opinion, then the Sukarno regime might always remain receptive to peaceful resolutions to international problems.[31] Indeed, it might even be influenced by American policy goals.

America's evidence of Sukarno's so-called moderate side could be traced to February 1962. In that month, Kennedy sent his brother, Attorney General Robert Kennedy, to Indonesia, requesting that Sukarno and the Dutch Foreign Minister, Joseph Luns, solve the West Irian matter at the conference table. Robert Kennedy was graciously received by the Indonesians, and Sukarno's ego was flattered by the younger Kennedy's attentions. This graciousness and attention did not assure a quick, peaceful solution. Foreign Minister Luns considered the United States a meddler in Dutch affairs. Serious negotiations did not begin until the spring of 1962 and only after the Kennedy administration made it clear that Holland could blame the United States for any New Guinea-related problem as long as the West Irian issue was resolved.[32]

During this period of uncertainty, an alleged "side issue" played a significant role in determining whether or not the new era of warmer United States–Indonesian relations was truly possible. Burying the past would be a fine symbolic gesture towards that opportunity. In November 1957, the Eisenhower administration approved a "special political action program" in Indonesia, offering American military assistance to the anti-communist, pro-West dissident movement of anti-Sukarno armed forces commanders in Sumatra and Celebes. This "program" included United States military air support. Publicly described by the Eisenhower administration as an independent "soldier of fortune," one of the American pilots, Allen Pope, was shot down by anti-aircraft fire while bombing a vessel in Ambon, Celebes. He was promptly captured by pro-Sukarno forces.

Pope was tried before an Indonesian Military Tribunal in December 1959 on various counts of aiding the enemies of Indonesia and bearing arms against Indonesia. On 29 April 1960, he was sentenced to death and the Indonesian Supreme Court upheld the decision in December 1960. This left him with only one option. He could appeal for presidential clemency and he did so at the time of the Kennedy–Sukarno meeting.

Throughout his trial and imprisonment, Pope stuck to his "soldier of fortune" cover story; however, by spring 1961 the Indonesians were well aware of official United States involvement in the events of the later 1950s. Howard Jones, the American Ambassador to Indonesia, sternly informed Sukarno that Pope's death would harm American–Indonesian relations. Consequently, his release remained in the interests of both countries.

Elvis Stahr, the American Secretary of the Army, took special interest in the case, keeping President Kennedy informed. The latter agreed with Stahr that Pope was "guilty as hell," but that America owed it to Pope to secure his release. The Pope matter became part of the Kennedy-Sukarno discussions, but the Indonesian leader offered no commitments. In early 1962, while in Indonesia, Robert Kennedy took a fresh approach to the case, noting that his brother's administration was not responsible for the "unfortunate" occurrences of the 1950s and that Pope's release would symbolize the "clean slate" that both governments needed to establish before embarking on a new era. Moreover, the Attorney General pointed out that the United States and the Soviet Union had both released downed pilots in recent months. Now, it was Indonesia's turn. This approach, combined with emotional appeals from Pope's wife and even Ambassador Jones, was successful. Sukarno released Pope, echoing the Kennedy administration's reasoning. Writing to President Kennedy in July 1962, Pope noted that "one realizes that mine was not an easy situation to resolve."[33] Indeed, the West Irian matter had already demonstrated that there was no "easy situation" in the American–Indonesian relationship.

The West Irian problem was finally resolved in August 1962. Following a series of long meetings between American, Dutch, and Indonesian officials, a United Nations interim government was arranged. Over an eight-month period, the United Nations would oversee the transfer of Dutch power to Indonesia, and in 1969 the local residents would decide whether to remain part of Indonesia. But, shortly before this agreement was reached, Kennedy was presented with yet another State Department position paper which concluded that Sukarno's sword-rattling over West Irian might be pure "showmanship." Deciding that the risks were too great to abandon the mediation efforts, Kennedy felt that in this case, "showmanship" and swift military action were qualities that Sukarno embraced.[34] The consequences of following through with the United States-inspired agreement were clear. Washington would be criticized by friends and foes for supporting Indonesian expansionism. On the other hand, the only alternative appeared to be war. The West Irian agreement was not a Pacific version of the old Munich conference. A possible Third World War over West Irian would be the ultimate folly, Kennedy believed. He remained steadfast in his approach, and the rhetoric concerning the new era of American-Indonesian friendship abounded.

The progress of this new era needed careful charting. Persuading Sukarno to solve longstanding economic problems and begin infrastructure development programs became a primary policy. Indonesia was faced with severe inflation and an adverse balance of payments. An increasingly unfavorable trade balance had resulted from a decline in earnings from rubber and petroleum. Foreign exchange reserves had fallen to the working balances of the commercial banks (estimated at $80 million). Meanwhile, Sukarno had drastically restricted imports, resulting in substantial cutbacks in production because of shortages or maldistribution of imported raw materials and spare parts. Industry was operating at only 30 to 40 per cent of capacity, and urban food supplies were inadequate.

Unless Indonesia dealt effectively with its own economic problems, Rusk told Kennedy, American assistance would be of little value. Meanwhile, it was obvious that the Soviet government was attempting to tie up future Indonesian exports through trade agreements and the acceptance of economic and military credits. By 1965, Rusk predicted, the Soviet government could shift the Indonesian trade pattern from the West to the Soviet Bloc.[35] Whether or not Indonesia used American aid properly, the State Department still preferred a massive aid program over none at all. The alternative, they believed, was an Indonesian government forced to lean on Soviet support.

Some Indonesian political leaders hoped to lure Sukarno away from Soviet temptations and compel him to take on growing domestic problems before it was too late. Kennedy planned to court them. For example, General Nasution was keenly aware that the Indonesian army was a drain on the overburdened economy. He desired an orderly demobilization in the interest of domestic development priorities. Against the army stood the Indonesian Communist Party, rapidly becoming the largest communist party outside of the Soviet Bloc. Between those forces was Sukarno. Unless he exercised what the State Department called "positive economic leadership" or delegated power on economic matters to competent ministers, the Soviets, Kennedy concluded, might eventually gain control of Indonesia's resources and the Communist Party would seize power.[36]

The Kennedy administration's reasoning for close Indonesian relations remained based on domino theory fears. "Our commitments on the Indo-China peninsula could be lost if the bottom of Southeast Asia fell out to Communism," Rusk wrote to Kennedy.

> It therefore remains our objective (1) to keep Indonesia independent and out of the Sino-Soviet camp, (2) to help Indonesia become a politically and economically viable nation, and (3) to help solve Indonesia's stabilization and recovery problems and eventually launch a national development plan.[37]

The State Department had not fully accepted the Kennedy thesis that war was inevitable over West Irian. The reason for a vigorous United States effort to achieve settlement of the West Irian issue, the State Department explained in an internal memorandum, "was that it would have an impact on the internal balance of political power."[38] Settlement would serve American interests because it would strengthen two groups in Indonesia, namely the army and a small but important group of non-leftist officials seriously interested in economic development.

The West Irian issue had truly dominated Indonesian politics, keeping the army preoccupied with military preparations and dependent on the communist bloc for support. Large military expenditures and exclusive political concentration on West Irian had also ruled out serious development effort. Furthermore, the communists had exploited the West Irian issue and Soviet support to strengthen their political position. A military attack would have accentuated all of these trends and seriously endangered the position of those who wanted to cooperate with the United States. When the settlement was achieved, the State Department planned to put it to "constructive use" by turning the attention of Indonesians away from militant nationalism and toward development, as well as by strengthening the army in the countryside. These were the two major elements of the State Department's long-term strategy to keep Indonesia noncommunist and to begin to give that country "some forward momentum."[39]

A Development Grant of $17 million, $32 million of rice (four times larger than any previous commitment), $40 million in wheat, flour, cotton and vegetable oil, a new patrol boat, T-37 jet trainers, and several multimillion dollar loans for industry and construction represented the specific "forward momentum" aspects of the new era.[40] Nevertheless, Kennedy thought more was needed on the ideological plane. The Indonesians, and Southeast Asians in general, deserved more than money thrown at them. A working symbol of the goodness of American policy was needed there, and the Peace Corps appeared to be the answer. No longer just an idea, the Peace Corps by late 1962 had already become a working agency and symbol of New Frontier foreign policy. Promising a lasting and positive American impact on Third World public opinion, the Peace Corps had caught the imagination of the world press. It became part of the elusive "right key" that Kennedy sought in achieving American policy goals and manipulating public opinion abroad.[41]

To Sukarno, the Peace Corps represented the type of commitment to peaceful relations that he admired in Kennedy. In 1963, he accepted twenty volunteers (mostly physical education teachers) as "symbols of the growing understanding and cooperation between our two nations."[42] They remained the largest contingent assigned to one Southeast Asian country. Aside from symbolism and high rhetoric, this did not mean that the new era had begun. By 1963 all sides in the West Irian dispute were relieved that a solution had been reached, but Sukarno felt he had been forced into a needless concession. Commenting on the United Nations mandate over West Irian, Sukarno accused the United Nations of frustrating the policies of developing nations such as Indonesia. He did not break the West Irian agreement, however.[43]

As the West Irian issue faded into obscurity, Sukarno took on another anti-colonial cause. The British government declared that it intended to grant independence (as one federated nation) to Malaya, Singapore, Sarawak and Sabah. Sukarno claimed that this new Malaysia was merely a foil for British imperialism. Indeed, the large presence of British military and commercial involvement after independence would make this claim at least tenable.

Kennedy saw no threat to Indonesia in the Malaysian idea, and he found Sukarno's "love of confrontation" annoying. In September 1963, Kennedy informed Sukarno that the Malaysia proposal was a peaceful one, offering the Malay nations a greater chance of successful development. Opposing the new Malaysia, Kennedy warned, "delayed the stabilization and development of the Indonesian economy." The new era was still possible, Kennedy promised, if Sukarno only recognized the peaceful intentions of the new Malaysia. Accenting this point, Kennedy proposed a special visit to Indonesia. The much-touted new era might formally begin, he implied, with this 1964 presidential visit.[44]

Sukarno was once again flattered by Kennedy's attention, but the Indonesian leader lived under a growing threat of assassination. As late as October 1963, a complicated plot on his life had been uncovered and the nearly successful May 1962 assassination attempt remained fresh in his mind. These latter concerns kept Sukarno in a justifiably suspicious mood when it came to both real and potential opponents. Although unfounded in this case, his suspicions sometimes included the United States.[45] This did little to create the new era, nor did threatening restrictions on soon-to-be-renegotiated American oil contracts in Indonesia. Kennedy appointed a special negotiator to Indonesia, Wilson Wyatt, to handle the restriction matter.[46] Sukarno knew Wyatt and enjoyed his company. Probably for that reason more than any other, Wyatt was successful in defending American oil interests.

The Kennedy administration attached great significance to the President's 1964 visit to Indonesia. Between March and late November 1963, Ambassador Jones, Roger Hilsman, the Assistant Secretary of State for Far Eastern Affairs, and Michael Forrestal, Senior Staff Member for the National Security Council directed all preparations for the event. Arguing that the Kennedy–Sukarno meeting must represent a turning point in American–Indonesian relations, they asked Kennedy to be blunt with Sukarno. Indonesia had not yet renounced any belligerent ambitions against its neighbors. If Indonesia promised to smooth things over with the Malaysians, Filipinos and others, the President, they said, must offer his administration's assistance. Should Indonesia agree, America would announce a new plan to stabilize the Indonesian economy. The specifics of the plan remained in rough draft form as late as 19 November 1963; however, the three policy-makers had definitely decided on a shipment of 150,000 tons of rice.[47]

The other specifics of the Jones–Hilsman–Forrestal plan depended on the visit of General Nasution. Scheduled to meet the President on Tuesday, 26 November 1963, Nasution planned to meet with Washington officials for a week. No one was sure why. Jones theorized that the Indonesian General wanted to explain the military's position on development before Kennedy met Sukarno. Since Nasution was a likely non-communist candidate to succeed Sukarno should the latter fall from power, Jones successfully lobbied for a brief Presidential appointment. In any event, Kennedy thought that he would have a better assessment of the current state of Indonesian politics thanks to the Nasution meeting. Hence, his administration was reluctant to conclude any specifics of the economic stabilization plan until after the General returned home.

But the Jones–Hilsman–Forrestal plan remained only one component of Kennedy's proposed mission to Djakarta. In March 1963, Sukarno had asked the Kennedy administration if its New Pacific Community idea was still alive and well. Kennedy avoided a direct answer to the question; however, it was apparent by November 1963 that the idea might have been alive but not well. He told Sukarno that American–Indonesian cooperation in solving the problems of Southeast Asia was possible. Yet, he questioned the correct path to success.

> As you know, it is our objective to assist the countries of Southwest and Southeast Asia to develop their economic and social institutions free from foreign subversion and domination. It is for this purpose that we have supported and cooperated with other nations with similar views to prevent the penetration of Chinese Communist power and to create and maintain the peace and security from fear which are essential if our common goal is to be reached. I hope that Indonesia, as the largest and the most powerful nation in Southeast Asia, will contribute to the common task of making it possible for all the free nations of Asia to develop in peace and security.[48]

Kennedy's comments coincided with the Diem assassination crisis and reflected an apparent, possibly temporary, backing away from the New Pacific Community formula. They also reflected a concern that Sukarno's days were numbered. In October 1963, the American Embassy in Indonesia reported that, given the number of Indonesians who would not mourn Sukarno's murder, "a betting man" might predict the future life span of the Indonesian leader to be "maybe less than a month."[49] Ironically, it was Kennedy who fell to an assassin's bullets one month later. Sukarno was deposed in a military-led coup that began in 1965. The vaguely defined new era never came about.

Despite its strong anti-communist goals, desire to maneuver nations in the interest of American policy, and forever influence the course of Southeast Asian development, the Kennedy administration maintained a lively and healthy dialogue with the Sukarno regime.

Since Sukarno was often viewed by American policy-makers as an obstruction to American influence in Southeast Asia and the Pacific, this peaceful dialogue in itself was a laudable achievement for Washington. The Kennedy administration's efforts to wed anti-communist priorities to allegedly noble and more idealogical endeavors, such as the New Pacific Community, were less laudable. The practical aspects of "the right key" in achieving basic American policy goals and winning the support of the Indonesians simply became larger aid packages, spiced with less than two dozen Peace Corps physical education teachers.

The fact that the Kennedy administration worked to improve America's approach to Indonesia and Southeast Asia represented a significant development in American foreign policy. Rhetoric over the proposed new era of American–Indonesian relations remained in the realm of wishful intentions; however, the time and energy spent by the Kennedy administration on Indonesian affairs indicated that Sukarno's conclusion concerning Kennedy's sincere desire for peaceful Indonesian–American relations was accurate. In spite of their different versions of democracy, Kennedy's New Frontier and Sukarno's Guided Democracy kept the peace between 1961 and 1963. Kennedy's New Pacific Community and the Yamin–Sukarno Federation of Malayan States illustrated how different those versions were. Most likely, Kennedy and Sukarno would have preferred to leave a more dramatic legacy of their relationship. But, given the already escalating violence in South Vietnam and Laos during the early 1960s, keeping the peace in at least one area of Southeast Asia was a dramatic and worthy exception to the rule.

5 "Holding the Beachhead" in the Philippines and Japan

The Kennedy administration had been confident of success in Indonesia, Australia, Micronesia, and elsewhere. Given these self-assurances, the Kennedy team worried that certain nations ("old friends") might be overlooked in the grand scheme of policy. According to Kennedy, when it came to Asian/Pacific relations, there were only two countries in this category of concern, Japan and the Philippines. The latter had already begun to advocate an anti-American position based both on neglect and national pride. Manila accused the Kennedy administration of avoiding economic development projects throughout America's former colony. Washington, some Filipinos said, favored projects in nations that did not enjoy the same historical ties to the United States. Coupled with this protest was a desire to separate the Philippines from American influences. Introducing new regulations for foreign investment, moving the national day from 4 July to the anniversary of the Philippines Revolution of 1898, and placing greater emphasis on the heroes of national history were just a few examples of the growing nationalist trend in the Philippines.[1]

To the Kennedy administration, the contradictory nature of Manila's new nationalism and anti-neglect campaign suggested that the Philippines needed greater focus in American foreign policy-making. Meanwhile, although it was still difficult for the United States government to call Japan a "friend," Kennedy worried that the Eisenhower administration had also taken American–Japanese relations for granted. American influences on local life and traditions remained as strong an issue in Tokyo as in Manila. Trade relations, the place of nuclear weapons in Kennedy's "massive retaliation" promise to thwart communism, and the future of the American military bases in Japan were major issues to the Japanese, threatening to delay the coming era of harmony in the New Pacific Community. In both the Philippines and Japan, Kennedy warned the cabinet in early 1961, America must "hold the beachhead."[2] The

Kennedy team needed no further instructions. Somehow, Tokyo and Manila were slipping from America's grasp. Considering the situation in Indochina and the desire to form the New Pacific Community, that grasp would have to be tightened.

Tightening-up American–Philippines relations was not an easy task. Despite the fact that American colonial authorities had encouraged democratic politics in the Philippines during the early decades of this century, Washington usually found Philippines politics confusing, corrupt, and not quite democratic. Political control in the Philippines had been in the hands of the Liberal Party from just before the date of independence (1946) until President Ramon Magsaysay bolted that Party and won election in November 1953 as leader of the second largest Party in the country, the Nacionalista. Killed in a plane crash during March 1957, Magsaysay was succeeded by the Vice President, Carols P. Garcia, a long-time member of the Nacionalista Party. After a heated campaign in which he was opposed by Jose Yulo of the Liberal Party, Manual Manahan of the Progressive Party, and Claro Recto of the Nationalist-Citizens Party, President Garcia won a plurality of 40 percent of the votes, thus retaining the Presidency for its constitutionally-mandated four-year term.[3]

By 1961, the State Department's verdict, as well as that of many Filipinos, was negative towards the Garcia administration. Garcia had failed to provide the purposeful, coordinated leadership necessary for an adequate sustained rate of economic growth, social reform, and corruption-free government. Although there was no militant threat to internal stability in 1961, public criticism and disgust with Garcia was widespread. In turn, Garcia attacked his critics for being either communist- or American-influenced. The attacks were haphazard, reflecting no conscious effort to embrace Sukarno-styled, non-alignment opinions. Nevertheless, Garcia's attacks on the use of English in the workplace and other American legacies drew some public attention away from socio-economic problems, stimulating enough support to prompt his re-election bid in the December 1961 elections. When Kennedy took office, Garcia's opposition appeared poised to take power later that year. The Vice President as well as Liberal Party chief, Diosdado Macapagal, was heavily favored to win. Consequently, the Kennedy administration planned to deal with both Garcia and Macapagal at the same time.[4]

During the New Pacific Community discussions, Kennedy rejected the idea of meeting Garcia personally. Ever conscious of symbols,

Kennedy considered Garcia an unfortunate product of American tolerance in the 1950s. He would not discuss the coming new era with a fading, corrupt symbol of the old.[5] This did not mean an end to friendly dialogue. Vice President Lyndon Johnson inherited the face-to-face role. Ordered to the Philippines in May 1961, Johnson was expected to discuss America's new interest in reform, economic development, Manila's role in Indochina, and the promising future. But was the Philippines ready for ambitious discussions and plans?

In spite of such fundamental elements of economic strength as sizeable natural resources, room for population expansion, increased agricultural production, and growing industrial plants, the Philippines shared many of the characteristics and problems common to Indonesia and other developing countries. Those problems and characteristics included dependence on a predominately agricultural economy, chronic trade deficits resulting in severe shortages of foreign exchange, a district lack of capital, and high rates of unemployment and under-development.

Nevertheless, the 1950s brought some economic progress to the Philippines thanks to United States assistance.[6] In spite of the ravages of the Japanese occupation and insurrection, post-war rehabilitation and expansion in the Philippines had been encouraging to the State Department. Between 1951 and 1960 the average annual growth in GNP ranged between 5 and 6 percent. The country's per capita GNP of $168 was one of the highest in Asia. Agricultural and industrial production had risen substantially during the early 1950s, but between 1956 and 1961 it had grown slightly faster than the increase in population of about 3 percent per annum.

Heartened by these figures, Rusk informed Kennedy that a special economic aid package could work in the Philippines. All it needed was a reliable administrator, but the current crop of Filipino politicians did not appear capable for the task. Claro Recto was especially annoying to Rusk. Recto's growing Nationalist-Citizen Party complained that American aid only fueled corruption. Manila's acceptance of even larger aid packages could be paid back, he stressed, only if Filipinos helped Americans kill fellow Southeast Asians in Vietnam. Recto advocated an isolationist policy in the name of Philippines "independence."

Recto's support could be quelled, Rusk argued, if Garcia and Macapagal were persuaded to work with America and avoid the temptations of corruption. Great things were possible, the State Department contended, if Manila permitted the economy to develop properly. Even under conditions of horrible fraud, waste, and mismanagement, the Philippines had reduced an external trade deficit of $182 million in 1957 to $10 million by 1961. Its balance-of-payments positions had improved as a result of various austerity and exchange measures, also providing a significant improvement in the Philippines's foreign exchange position. This fact, combined with Garcia's 1961 peso devaluation legislation, added further stimulus to the economy and promised price stability for at least a year.[7]

There was always room for hope. Johnson's mission to the Philippines was based on the fact that both the U.S and the Philippine government had little desire to encourage communist growth anywhere in Asia, including the Philippines. The latter, with American assistance, had halted the communist-supported "Huk" revolt only one decade earlier. Certainly, the Kennedy cabinet reasoned, Manila was aware of the attraction of communism to the impoverished. Hence, the Garcia government would welcome America's interests in economic development, regional security, and cooperation.[8] Yet, Kennedy remained reluctant to initiate specific aid packages or defense arrangements with Manila. Johnson left for the Philippines with plenty of talking points, but few resolutions to the problems at hand. Once again, the Kennedy administration indicated its difficulty in grappling with the complications of Third World politics. Once again, the vision of an American-inspired prosperity and peace clouded immediate policy objectives.

The Philippines had played an active and generally constructive role in the United Nations, and its major foreign policy goals substantially supported those of the United States. But Recto's argument was beginning to influence the Garcia government in the spring of 1961. Felixberto Serrano, the Secretary of Foreign Affairs, told Johnson that the situation in Laos and Vietnam demonstrated the ineffectiveness of SEATO and American power. The United States, he said, overestimated its power to influence events in the capitals and countrysides of the Southeast Asian nations. Manila, he predicted, would soon be forced to shore-up relations with all neighboring states because of this American "weakness."[9]

Johnson labeled Serrano an "extreme chauvinist" for his opinion. He expected support for Indochina policy, not defeatism. Serrano's reasoning, Johnson concluded, was based on the lack of information. Washington, he promised, would never neglect its duty to keep an ally informed. He promised new communications links for the new era of American–Philippines cooperation.

We intend to consult and cooperate fully with the Philippines and our other SEATO allies in planning for future contingencies or actions affecting SEATO and its responsibilities. We continue to regard SEATO's role as vital to the security of Southeast Asia.[10]

Johnson not only quickly dismissed Serrano's keen perception of events, he exaggerated the misinformation issue. John Hickerson, the American Ambassador to Manila, insisted that the Foreign Office was always well-informed; however, he was not sure what happened to American cables once they arrived there. Like Johnson, Hickerson hailed from Texas, and the two, at least in public, got along famously in Manila. Hickerson stressed simple, basic points when discussing Philippines affairs with Johnson. According to Hickerson, Manila's confusion over the proper relaying of American information was representative of government in the Philippines. Gossip, patronage, and rumor were its better characteristics.[11]

Under these cirumstances, could America "hold the beachhead" and plan for the future? Johnson thought so, and apparently considered Hickerson a good buddy who was becoming much too cynical for his own good. Johnson hoped to explain the New Frontier to the Filipinos and return home with a foundation for agreement on several issues: civil air negotiations, war damage assistance, military bases, and miliary assistance. Johnson considered this foundation tantamount to direct and active support for American policy in general, including all actions in Vietnam and Laos.[12] Once laid, the foundation would lead to the New Pacific Community and perhaps a new breed of Filipino politicians.

As in the case of Australia, the Kennedy administration slowly realized that there were certain issues, deemed minor by Washington, that were often more important to a sparring partner than visions of the future. In the Philippines, America's sugar quota was one of those issues, and it did nothing to enlighten Washington–Manila relations. President Eisenhower's defense of the quota had prompted major anti-American demonstrations in Manila during 1956. The American Congress's ignoring of Philippine sugar concerns in favor of Cuban sugar interests during the waning days of the Batista regime also disturbed relations. Yet, the Kennedy administration still did not see the issue as a significant one, and instructed Johnson to ignore it.[13] This also proved to be a difficult assignment.

The sugar quota issue dated back to 1946. In that year, the United States–Philippines Trade Agreement set the annual sugar quota from the Philippines at 952,000 short tons. The Revised Trade Agreement of 1955 retained this figure, and all post-war United States sugar legislation had incorporated the Trade Agreement quota. The Philippines was the only area, foreign or domestic, that remained subject to an absolute quota. As such, its proportionate share of the growing United States sugar market had declined year-by-year. The Philippines government had consistently pressed for an increase in their nation's basic quota, suggesting to the new Kennedy administration that Filipino patience had been tried too long.[14]

Arriving in Manila on 8 May 1961, Johnson was told by Ambassador Hickerson that sugar was the top item on their host government's agenda. Given the minor place that Philippines sugar played in American politics, he wanted the Vice President to persuade his colleagues in Congress not to legislate sugar windfalls for their friends in the domestic sugar industry. Obviously, that legislation would be to the detriment of the Philippines. But the powers of persuasive politics were more easily accomplished in Manila than in Washington. Johnson explained that he had no authority over Congressional government procedure, and that the Philippines had enjoyed a larger share of the American sugar market since the breaking of relations with Castro's sugar-rich Cuba. Indeed, one of Eisenhower's last acts as President had been to announce a non-quota allocation of 341,000 tons from the Philippines for 1961. Johnson promised to offer the same figure for 1962.[15]

Garcia complained that Kennedy's continuation of the quota was based on "prejudice." Not meaning to infer a racial problem, Garcia believed that the quota "prejudiced" local economic development and he stressed the point. Noting that he expected more from the New Frontier, Garcia criticized the Kennedy administration for following through Eisenhower's sugar policy. Johnson insisted that America never viewed the Philippines with "prejudice," but that the sugar matter was "deserving" of a Congressional hearing.[16] It was his final word on the matter.

As far as Johnson and the Kennedy administration were concerned, the Philippine sugar quota was generous and fair. Any special treatment for Manila would be considered after the Filipinos demonstrated their competence to rule and stand firm against communist growth in the region. Given the state of Philippines politics, the New Pacific Community remained an elusive goal there. But, Johnson was a dogged negotiator. He left Manila convinced that the Philippines was not slipping into apathy on Cold War matters, moving toward the non-aligned states, or even suffering from interminable corruption. In general, Johnson concluded, the Filipinos continued to support an American vision of the world. All they needed was a close watching, perhaps even guidance. Paraphrasing FDR, whom Johnson called his "political papa," the tired Vice President denounced the Filipinos as a bunch of SOBs. But, they are "our SOBs," he added.[17]

Winning Manila's support on his key agenda items was proof enough to the Vice President that there was a happy future for American–Filipino relations. Civil Air negotiations, for instance, had promised problems, yet the issue was smoothed over easily. Since the Philippines terminated the 1946 United States–Philippines Air Transport Agreement in 1960, American airlines (Pan American and Northwest) had continued to serve Manila under periodic extensions of temporary permits granted by the Philippine government. When Kennedy took office, negotiations for a new agreement were at an impasse. Garcia insisted on inclusion of a Tokyo stop for its flag carrier (PAL) when the latter resumed trans-Pacific service to the United States. Citing "aviation economics" and American government concerns over PAL's poor safety standards and equipment malfunctions, Eisenhower had opposed the expansion of PAL flights. Johnson suggested that frequent air transport service between the United States and the Philippines was "in the deepest interest of both countries." President Kennedy, he said, planned to review the situation personally. Despite continued opposition by American aviation experts, Johnson suggested that a Tokyo inclusion and the resumption of full PAL services was a simple matter. As long as Northwest and Pan American airlines were freed from the temporary permit restrictions, Johnson saw no difficulties ahead.[18]

Rhetoric over the coming era of jet age communications and transportation between the two countries abounded at the Johnson–Garcia meeting. It only benefited the positive, New Pacific Community atmosphere that the Kennedy administration wanted to impress upon the Garcia government. But, Kennedy still doubted that the Philippines was as capable as Australia and other nations in playing a fruitful role in the New Pacific Community. At best, it appeared destined to play a backseat role in both military and development crusades elsewhere in the region.[19] Fifteen years after the declaration of Philippines independence, the American government viewed the Philippines as a struggling child of American colonialism.[20]

One way to ease that struggle, and inject some needed life into

Washington–Manila relations, was to resolve the lingering problem of World War II damage claims. According to the Romulo–Synder Agreement of 1950, the United States and the Philippines planned to settle all matters of loans and compensations related to World War II within a decade's time. In early 1961, the Garcia government offered a payment of $20 million to the United States, thereby setting its Romulo–Snyder loan repayment obligations. Garcia expected the United States to move immediately on the payment of $73 million in war damage claims to his government, thereby ending its obligations as well.[21]

Philippines politics complicated the war claims issue. The House of Representatives in Manila passed a resolution demanding $81 million from the United States above the $73 million noted by Garcia. This $154 million claim, the resolution pointed out, was "just and reasonable." The resolution was written in frustration over the failure of the Philippines Economic Mission to the United States. Originally sent to Washington in 1955, the Mission, for the next several years, presented lists of claims for American compensation funds. A large proportion of the lists deal with payments to Filipino veterans who either served with American forces or fought as guerrillas during World War II. Other claims included those arising from the reduction of the weight of the gold dollar in 1934, adjustments under the specific loan provisos of Romulo–Synder, requests for refunds of processing taxes, and property damage complaints.

Extensive studies by the Departments of Treasury, Defense, and State between 1955 and 1961 resulted in the decision that no legal or equitable basis existed for most of the claims. There was only one exception. During August 1959, a payment of $23,862,751 was offered on the claims resulting from the devaluation of the dollar in 1934. Meanwhile, the Kennedy administration even disagreed with Garcia's figure of $73 million, noting that the figure was "probably" too high.[22] The United States Congress supported the President and offered its own protest of the $73 million claim. It set a limit of 75 percent as the maximum which might be paid on any approved claim amounting to more than $500.

The Philippines Congress protested that the New Frontier planned to stifle their nation's economic rehabilitation. They urged Garcia and Macapagal to stand tall against "American tyranny." Garcia stuck to his $73 million figure. Ever cautious of the political winds, Macapagal declared his "neutrality." Although he was not sure how Garcia arrived at the $73 million, Johnson said that he supported the payment. Cautiously, he explained that the American Congress might arrive at a lower figure, but that the Kennedy administration "remained committed to the postwar growth of the economy of the Philippines."[23]

Indeed, Kennedy set aside his "concern" over Garcia's figure. He asked for and received legislation that added $73 million to the foreign assistance authorization for the Philippines. Sponsored by Clement Zablocki on the House Foreign Affairs Committee, the War Damage Bill stimulated heated debate over America's policy towards the Philippines. The debate never questioned America's effort to maneuver the Philippines into a strongly pro-American, anti-communist position, but it did question the cost of the effort. Hailing from Milwaukee's largely Polish-American "South Side," Zablocki, a World War II veteran, had nothing to gain for his district. If the $73 million strengthened American–Filipino relations, he argued, then the President deserved the Congress's support. His colleagues eventually agreed. On 30 August 1962, Kennedy signed the legislation into law.

> This legislation makes it possible for the United States to fulfill the obligations voluntarily undertaken by us at the close of World War II in recognition of the common sacrifices made by the Philippine and American people. The war caused enormous damage to the Philippine Islands. The payments under this bill, together with the $400 million already appropriated, will help repair that damage. I am particularly gratified that the legislation provides that the amounts paid will, to a large extent, be reinvested in the Philippines economy.[24]

Whereas $473 million constituted one of the America's most expensive Asian aid packages in history, it was defense-related matters that immediately concerned the Kennedy team. Hickerson had already begun negotiations on military basing privileges when Johnson arrived in May 1961. The Vice President was expected to speed the process and establish the cooperative framework needed for defense relations in the New Pacific Community. The arguments, Johnson soon discovered, were not about weapons, training or even construction. Instead, the American–Filipino discussions were stalemated over problems in local law, politics, and pride.

The United States operated four major bases and several minor installations in the Philippines under a 1947 Military Base Agreement. These bases were deemed essential to the defense of the

Western Pacific area. "A mutually satisfactory revision of the out-dated 1947 Agreement," Rusk once informed Johnson, "would doubtless improve the psychological climate in which we must oper-ate the bases."[25] In August 1959, the United States had already relinquished large portions of several "non-essential" military reser-vations to the Manila government. At the same time, Manila permit-ted the Americans to extend the acreage of select bases as well as make use of bases previously reserved for the armed forces of the Philippines. Finally, in December 1959, the United States Navy relinquished control over the town of Olongapo, adjacent to Amer-ica's Subic Bay Naval Station. The "return of Olongapo" had been a battle cry of Philippines politicians since 1946.[26]

When Kennedy took office, the American government had prom-ised to (1) consult with the Philippines government before using the bases in regional military action, (2) consult before installing long range missiles, (3) shorten the original base agreement from 99 to 25 years pending a new agreement, and, (4) defend the Philippines in case of attack. Problems remained in the areas of criminal jurisdic-tion over American military personnel and how to properly implement local laws on the bases. The Garcia government demanded full respect for local law both on- and off-base. A final agreement on America's continuing role in the Philippines, he said, depended on Washington's recognition of that law. Consequently, the matter became an intensely political one, forcing Garcia to pub-licly demand America's respect for Philippine law.

The status of forces agreements on criminal jurisdiction in the NATO countries and Japan did not apply to the Philippines. Those agreements constituted a working compromise on legal rights *vis-à-vis* American bases. Manila did not support compromises. In fact, Garcia took the very suggestion of compromise as an insult to the integrity of the Philippines. Manila, he argued, could never accept the same type of deal offered to "ex-enemy countries" (Germany and especially Japan). It was full control or nothing.

Because Garcia had committed himself publicly to the full control position, it would be difficult for him to back away from it if America revised its argument. Johnson, who considered himself a master of the New Deal-styled political deal, went to Manila prepared to woo Garcia from the hard line. Taking over from Hickerson's straightfor-ward approach, Johnson invited the Philippines to write its own jurisdiction procedure as long as it was in "harmony" with the arrangements made in Japan and the NATO nations. Since "harmony" was not to be defined by the Philippines, the Johnson approach permitted the Garcia government to back away from the hard line and enact a jurisdiction procedure that resembled the status quo elsewhere. Foreign Secretary Serrano welcomed the formula and persuaded Garcia to move on it.[27] The legal mechanics of Philippines jurisdiction over base matters took months to conclude, but Johnson had opened a door to cooperation that had not existed before.

Ranging from his days as an administrative assistant for a Texas Congressman before the New Deal to his position as Senate Majority Leader in the late 1950s, Johnson had demonstrated his skill in the cloakroom tactics of Capitol Hill. The Kennedy brothers had selected him for the Vice Presidential slot because of that skill and because his state represented a key to victory in the 1960 election. Successfully calling in his IOUs from the Democratic Party leadership and delivering Texas to the Kennedy team, Johnson, as far as the President was concerned, had already fulfilled his major obligations as Vice President before he took the oath of office.[28]

The Kennedy administration, and particularly Attorney General Kennedy, remained suspicious of Johnson's commitment to New Frontier interests, such as in the field of civil rights/civil liberties. The suspicions were misplaced, for Johnson's record on a variety of domestic reform issues was respectable and obvious. This success, inspired by his admiration for the humanist mission of specific New Deal efforts to remedy the Great Depression, separated him from the conservative, segregationist wing of the Southern Democratic Party. His willingness to wheel-and-deal with that wing to achieve results in legislation confused the Kennedys. The latter often found eloquent but cautiously presented statements on behalf of reform more acceptable to the electorate than legislative success based on compromise, schemes, and deals.

Their tactics differed, but the President and his Vice President agreed that the New Deal deserved a certain modernization. To Kennedy, it was the intellectual yet pragmatic New Frontier. To Johnson, it would be the activist Great Society. Both believed that they acted in the best interests of the FDR legacy. Given Johnson's political skill and ambition, his choice as envoy to the Philippines in 1961 was a good one. Nevertheless, Johnson's folksy manner and rough Texas politics suggested to some that he had no business dealing with the intricacies of Asian international relations.[29] In reality, Johnson was as capable a diplomat as Kennedy. The Philippines mission proved the point. He welcomed the general New Frontier thesis in foreign affairs and its specific New Pacific Community expression. Between 1961 and late 1963, there was nothing in the realm of solid evidence to indicate that he was more or less of a "hawk" than Kennedy in the military aspects of foreign policy-making.

Indeed, Washington–Manila military affairs played a major part in Johnson's 1961 mission to the Philippines. Despite the corruption, proven misuse of American military aid, and the shaky position of democracy in the Philippines, Kennedy believed that the Eisenhower administration had been too frugal when it came to the Military Assistance Program (MAP) for Manila. Always concerned about Pacific security, Kennedy considered the Philippines "our arsenal of democracy in the Pacific."[30] FDR had declared America the "arsenal of democracy" during Britain's days of siege by Hitler's air forces in World War II. There was no easy comparison of Churchill's Britain to Garcia's Philippines, but the Kennedy administration saw the communist threat in Southeast Asia in the same dangerous light as Nazi expansionism in the early 1940s. With that point in mind, plus the American military tradition in "Fortress Philippines" at Corregidor, Camp John Hay, and Clark Field before World War II, Kennedy's call to action reminded the cabinet of America's historical ties with Manila.

But arming the Philippines would take time. Garcia had several complaints against the MAP and he demanded specific weapons systems. The Philippines, Garcia noted, lagged behind other American allies in the area of "modern defensive weapons." No nation could debate the future of the Pacific region in the new Pacific Community, he told Johnson, until it could adequately defend itself. To Garcia, "modern defensive weapons" meant short-range surface-to-air missiles which were capable of being armed with nuclear warheads in time of emergency. Garcia was well-aware that the United States furnished NIKE missiles to Taiwan under the MAP, and he submitted a proposal to Johnson calling for twice as many missiles as Taiwan. Johnson explained that "the ground environment" (special training and maintenance capability) did not exist in the Philippines. The proposal would take many years to implement, he warned. Garcia ignored the warning and stood his ground.

Johnson's warnings only fueled Garcia's second major complaint. The Philippines, he said, needed a voice in the programming of United States military assistance. In a long and polite fashion, Johnson explained that programming was the responsibility of the executive and legislative branches of the American government. The Kennedy administration, he promised, would happily consult with Manila on the programming process, but it would never permit the direct involvement of the Garcia government in that process.

Apparently annoyed with Johnson's answers, Garcia accused the Kennedy administration of deliberately delaying delivery of tanks, howitzers, and other weapons authorized during the Eisenhower administration. Johnson pointed out that Garcia's weapons list was exaggerated. There was only one active Philippines Army division, and it had received its MAP authorization. Otherwise, Johnson promised an on-time delivery of several all-weather interceptor F86D aircraft in the summer of 1961.[31]

Whereas Garcia defined Philippines defense in the area of nuclear weapons and the latest technology, Kennedy defined it as rooted in America's response to communist growth.[32] Kennedy preferred a well-equipped, well-trained Philippines Army that enjoyed a good salary and adequate living conditions. In short, he dreamed of an American-modelled force that would be reliable to America in nearby brushfire wars. It would also function in a truly democratic state. Like many dreams, it was unlikely to come true. Kennedy thought it inappropriate to fund the creation, training, and very life of the Philippines armed forces. The Garcia government, he said, must contribute something to the effort if the cooperative framework of the New Pacific Community was to become reality. Kennedy had four active divisions in mind for the army alone. Improvements to the naval and air forces would come later. Johnson relayed the message, but Garcia refused to contribute one peso. It was America's responsibility, he concluded. Macapagal agreed.[33]

The MAP discussion ended the Garcia–Johnson talks. Johnson recommended to Kennedy that America freeze its MAP for the Philippines until Manila demonstrated its effective use of past and present assistance. The Vice President's opinion was matched in a lengthy study conducted by staff aides to the House Foreign Affairs Committee. Given this advice, Kennedy gave up on his dream of the Philippines as the active democratic partner.[34] It was only May 1961.

Without question, the dream had been complicated by the realities of Philippines politics. Garcia's "thank you" letter to the White House, complimenting Johnson on his diplomacy, did not help. Garcia asked for more American aid, and in an area that he had not even discussed with Johnson.

We want to update and improve our education in science and technology to carry us forward and upward in our industrialization program. Our laboratories and equipment in colleges and universities and vocational schools are in woeful need of modernization. It is my hope that the Philippines will receive what we initially need to make us the most industrially and scientifically developed country in Asia. We would like also to make full use of your Peace Corps project, specially to inject more vigor into our community development program. This is the kind of project that will touch the grassroots of democracy in the Philippines.[35]

For the rest of his administration, Kennedy viewed the Philippines with the long-term in mind. Concern over the Kennedy legacy and the possibilities of the New Pacific Community was nothing new to this administration; however, Philippines affairs was seen as painful business throughout most of 1961 and 1962. By 1963, the effects of Kennedy's economic assistance program to the Philippines were beginning to take shape. Macapagal, as predicted, became President at the end of 1961. He even planned to visit the White House during the summer of 1962, but he was forced to cancel his plans. Dozens of American Congressmen had protested the proposed visit, noting that "the Filipinos were coming for another handout." Macapagal blamed the "present climate in the United States" for the cancellation.[36] By early 1963, the Kennedy aid was being spent and Macapagal admitted to Washington the he "hoped" it was being used properly.[37]

In the interest of assuring future aid agreements, and with the promise that his government was spending American money for the benefit of the Philippine people, Macapagal appointed Rufino G. Hechanova, the Secretary of Commerce and Industry, to discuss money matters with the Kennedy administration. Hechanova was expected to complete his work between July and December 1963. Kennedy was interested in Hechanova's report on existing spending levels and accounts; however, the Filipino politician was more adept at petitioning for new aid plans. Kennedy granted one of Hechanova's wishes and it dated back to Garcia's "thank you" letter of May 1961. He asked Congress to approve a small higher education exchange program for the Philippines.[38]

This was not the new era of warm, cooperative relations that Macapagal had promised would result from the Hechanova mission. The American–Filipino dialogue continued, but there were few differences between its late 1963 and early 1961 versions. Meanwhile, the Manila government was nearly $500 million richer, and the Kennedy administration saw no serious reform effort of either the economy or the defense structure. Washington was still "holding the beachhead;" however, it could claim little else.

The new breed of Filipino politicians that Kennedy hoped the New Frontier would encourage to power liked his style, but not his message. Representing what the Manila press called "The New Politics," Senate President Ferdinand Marcos was young, a Kennedy-compared hero of World War II, and a clever politician. Switching from the Liberal to the Nacionalista Party, Marcos played the "old politics" extremely well.[39] He positioned himself in the early 1960s to run against Macapagal in the 1965 elections. Moreover, between 1961 and 1965, Marcos asked the electorate innumerable questions about their expectations of democracy, employing a campaign technique reminiscent of Kennedy's 1960 campaign of promise and hope. Unlike Kennedy, Marcos never attempted to answer the questions that he posed.

> For the Filipino, especially, revolution is self-examination In his heart he knows that in the democratic setting where he has lived all his life, he has come to a point of crisis where the institutions conceived to protect his freedom, fulfill his hopes, and redress the injustices he may suffer have failed. . . . Faced by these failures of his democracy, frustrated to the point of despair by the callousness of the powerful, but filled nevertheless with a longing for a better life, what can the Filipino do?[40]

The problems of American relations with Japan, the other "beachhead," differed from American–Filipino relations, but proved equally as frustrating to the Kennedy administration. As in so many areas of policy, Kennedy noted in early 1961 that America's relationship to Japan promised "new beginnings."[41] Signed just months before Kennedy took office, the Mutual Security Treaty with Japan symbolized this "new beginning." The treaty revised an earlier agreement of 1951, assuring the continuation of the American military presence in Japan. Significantly, the treaty recognized Japan, and not the Philippines, as the most important strategic link in America's Pacific security system.[42]

This special recognition, plus basing privileges, created an outcry of anti-Americanism throughout Japan. Furthermore, the very fact that the Japanese government planned to revise its defense relationship with Washington stimulated greater public debate in Japan during the 1950s than the specific provisos of the treaty itself. The 1951 agreement had only requested "consultation" between the two governments in the event of military action. Many Japanese felt that this type of wording did not commit the United States to the defense of Japan. The new treaty compared an attack on Japan as significant as an attack on the United States, requiring an immediate American response. Basing privileges were guaranteed throughout the 1960s, but deployment from those bases included full Japanese consultation. Prime Minister Nobusuke Kishi considered this successful inclusion of his government's wishes as representative of "America's new recognition of Japanese pride and honor."[43] The electorate did not agree.

Communists, socialists, neutralists, and even moderate critics of Kishi's Liberal Party saw the treaty as Japanese entrapment in the Cold War. Some attacked it for not including the return of the American-occupied Ryukyu Islands to Japan. Others noted the lack of a Japanese veto over American deployment of nuclear weapons on the bases. Others thought the special recognition of Japan in the American security link invited attack from the Soviet Union and mainland China. And many others simply opposed another decade of the American presence.[44]

Distrust of post-war American intentions ran deep. The *Lucky Dragon* incident was a case in point. During 1954, the crew of the Japanese fishing boat, *Lucky Dragon*, suffered from radioactive fallout while sailing in the vicinity of a Marshall Islands nuclear test. The Eisenhower administration offered $2 million to the families of the dying crew, but the issue led to Japanese street demonstrations as well as denunciations from the *Diet*, Japan's Parliament, concerning America's reckless use of nuclear weapons.[45] The memories of Hiroshima and Nagasaki were fresh in mind throughout Japan. Tokyo's opposition to America's nuclear arsenal would remain a mainstay of Japanese political life.

Meanwhile, anti-Americanists were heartened by success over the Girard affair of 1957. William Girard, an American soldier, shot and killed a Japanese woman while she foraged for scrap metal on an American firing range. Abiding by the Status of Forces Agreement of 1952, the American military surrendered Girard to the Japanese authorities. Thanks to pressure from an outraged United States Congress, the military attempted to regain jurisdiction. William Knowland, the Senate Republican leader, spearheaded the effort, proclaiming that American servicemen must be safeguarded from foreign law and foreigners in general. Knowland's crusade spurned anti-American demonstrations in Japan as well as an American Supreme Court decision on the legal viability of status of forces agreements. Chief Justice Earl Warren declared those agreements legally valid. Hence, Girard was tried in a Japanese court, sentenced to three years in a Japanese jail, but then promptly released.[46] The entire issue offered the Japanese government a sense of pride in their successful challenge of America in the name of justice. To the anti-American demonstrators, the issue offered a precedent for success against the larger matter at hand, the Mutual Security Treaty.

Kishi had hoped Eisenhower would visit Japan before he left office, and he invited him to do so in June 1960. Violent demonstrations, many of them sponsored by the Socialist Party, the major opposition party, led to Kishi's cancellation of the visit. Sadly, he admitted that his government could not assure the President's safety. But Eisenhower had already left on an Asian countries tour. Consequently, the cancellation brought embarrassment to the soon-to-retire American President, and it bolstered the non-alignment cause in Asia. Kishi's government fell largely because of the cancellation flap. It was replaced by another Liberal government headed, this time, by Hayato Ikeda. Eloquent and pragmatic, Ikeda promised to stand firm on Japanese interests in the treaty as well as on government plans to accelerate economic growth in the 1960s. The Japanese electorate appeared persuaded by Ikeda's tough rhetoric, and many anti-American demonstrators were happy and satisfied with Kishi's fall.[47] For Washington, this meant the Mutual Security Treaty would remain intact. For Tokyo, it meant a quieting of anti-American zeal and the promise of a working relationship with the new American President, John Kennedy.

As in the case of the Philippines, Kennedy worried that divisive politics in Japan might eventually undermine American security interests.[48] Yet, the major Philippines issues of corruption and development assistance did not apply to Tokyo. "Holding the beachhead" in Japan always involved keeping the Mutual Security Treaty alive, allaying Japanese fears over American nuclear diplomacy, encouraging free trade while discouraging protectionist measures in Congress, and promising full cooperation and a happy future in the New Pacific Community.

Whereas many Americans considered Japan a defeated World War II nation and post-war manufacturer of trinkets and toys, the

Japanese viewed themselves as a rising power on the international scene.[49] Ikeda declared that Japan sought to develop its own distinctive role in foreign affairs during the 1960s. Growing Japanese economic interest in Southeast Asia proved the point. In the late 1950s, specific reparations deals with former Japanese occupied territories in Southeast Asia opened the door to future investment. That future was complicated by Peking's interest in the region and by the fact that Japanese–Chinese relations remained weak. Efforts to improve the Peking–Tokyo dialogue in 1962 and 1963 were supported by both governments, but collapsed while mainland China contemplated its role in the deteriorating Vietnam situation. Meanwhile, as early as February 1961, the Ikeda government announced that Japan's postwar economic debts to America would soon be paid. That final payment would be made during the Kennedy administration's tenure. Indeed, Robert Kennedy, on his way to meet Sukarno during the West Irian crisis, was in Tokyo at the time of the payment. Without question, Ikeda successfully championed the issue of Japanese pride and prestige. Although he never sought Japan's independence from American ties, a Soviet–Japanese trade agreement in 1962 indicated that Japan was truly serious about breaking away from post-war isolation.[50]

Japan's international ambitions did not stimulate the New Pacific Community. Kennedy's Japanese policy would be caught between two powerful forces. On the one hand, Congress demanded a protectionist slap at Japan's lingering anti-Americanism. On the other hand, the Kennedy cabinet wanted Japan's active support in anticommunist causes throughout Southeast Asia. American and Japanese economic investments in the region should be coordinated, Rusk noted during the New Pacific Community discussions.[51] As always, the specifics behind this coordinated effort were not defined. And, as always, Kennedy preferred a working relationship with the given nation before suggesting the so-called happy partnership in the New Pacific Community. But would Congress support this partnership if the Japanese electorate continued to express its anti-Americanism? Was the partnership possible considering that sentiment?

The answers to these questions depended on Kennedy's handling of protectionist legislation and on whether or not the "new beginnings" rhetoric of both Kennedy and Ikeda could translate into agreements on specific matters of joint concern. Between January and May 1961, Kennedy was faced with several protectionist resolutions and bills from Congress. Targeting Japan, these measures noted Japan's growing dependence on an export economy. They also declared America's interest in economic self-defense before these exports posed a threat to domestic industry.

Representatives John Baldwin and Leo W. O'Brien offered the most controversial legislation. Both men were members of Kennedy's Democratic Party; the Party that reversed the Smoot–Hawley tariff and other protectionist measures during the early 1930s. Thus, Baldwin and O'Brien's legislation was rooted more in nationalist, anti-Japanese fervor than Democratic Party tradition. In any event, Kennedy had never expressed any diehard loyalty to free trade practices. His judgement on the matter would be based on priorities in foreign policy-making rather than economic thought.

Baldwin proposed legislation that required a modification of Executive Order 10582, forbidding the American government to purchase any Japanese product for any of its agencies, including the military. Kennedy noted that the Buy American Act already prohibited the government from purchasing foreign products unless the prices for domestic goods were "unreasonable." Executive Order 10582 was a procurement measure, largely devoted to modernizing government offices with the latest and best equipment. Kennedy saw the Baldwin Bill as not only an open door to a protectionist era, but also an attack on Executive Order privilege. In his 6 February 1961 message to Congress, Kennedy lashed out at the Baldwin Bill and protectionism in general. "A return to protectionism," he insisted, "is not a solution. Such a course could result in retaliation abroad with serious consequences for U.S. exports and our trade balance."[52]

One month later, he accused Baldwin of injuring American–Japanese diplomacy, harming executive-legislative relations, and dividing Democrats. He asked him to drop the cause. The Congressman obliged, but his Bill was quickly replaced by an even more obvious anti-Japanese measure. Representative O'Brien, an old Kennedy supporter and ally in most areas of legislation, sponsored a Bill "to observe December 7th each year as 'the day that will live in infamy.' " The Bill suggested that a national holiday was required to honor the American dead of the recent Pacific War, noting that the President himself was almost killed in that conflict. Furthermore, the Bill implied that the Japanese had not yet repented for the Pearl Harbor attack and other World War II actions. Anti-American sentiment in Japan was used as a fine testament to the fact. Kindness to Japan's export economy, the Bill proclaimed, must not be forthcoming.[53]

With Prime Minister Ikeda due to visit the White House at the end of June 1961, Kennedy wanted his anti-protectionist position well-established. Since his accusations against Baldwin had not halted the flow of anti-Japanese measures from Capitol Hill, Kennedy's rhetoric became stronger. On 4 May 1961, he announced that he would never support anti-Japanese protection. He reserved a special rebuke for O'Brien.

> I suppose that all of us feel the same about December 7, 1941. However, we are now trying to *improve* Japanese–American relationships, and I doubt that calling the Japanese names each year is calculated to achieve that purpose.[54]

The O'Brien Bill failed.

In contrast to the other Pacific state visits to the White House, Ikeda's trip was a late one. Now skilled in the art of head-to-head dialogue, Kennedy led the discussion, keeping his comments brief and to the point. On the issue of consultation, Kennedy promised immediate discussions with the Ikeda government on any future matter of policymaking relevance. To illustrate the point, he briefed the Japanese Prime Minister on the latest round of American–Soviet communications over Berlin and Laos. On trade, he explained that the protectionists had lost in Congress. The present and the future, he promised, was a liberal trade policy towards Japan. As for nuclear weapons and China, Kennedy treated these distinct issues in a similar fashion, noting America's respect for Japan's fear of nuclear war and its desire to make amends with an old enemy, China. Kennedy insisted that consultation would eliminate any questions Japan had over America's nuclear arsenal. China, he said, threatened both American and Japanese economic interests in Asia. That threat justified democratic opposition to a Chinese delegation at the United Nations as well as America's support of the Republic of China.[55]

Ikeda welcomed Kennedy's candor on all points except China. Non-recognition, he said, fostered tensions that could lead to nuclear war. Yet, he stated his opposition to communism and noted that Peking was a "confusing" state with militant ambitions. Ikeda added only one additional issue to the agenda, the Ryukyus. The Prime Minister pointed out that the Americans consistently ignored the significance of the issue to 1960s relations. Indeed, Kennedy had hoped to avoid the matter in favor of discussion points that met mutual agreement. He concluded the discussion on that point, reserving the Ryukyus for "special considerations" later. Outlining the New Pacific Community, Kennedy declared that no issue could truly divide American–Japanese friendship in the 1960s. Ikeda responded with a polite bow.[56]

Ikeda left Washington without a precise definition of what American–Japanese friendship entailed in the 1960s. Kennedy's progress in stemming the tide of protectionism appeared to be laying the finest foundation for 1960s Japanese–American cooperation. In fact, the staffs of the two leaders worked out a proposal to establish the Joint United States–Japan Committee on Trade and Economic Affairs. This cabinet level Committee was officially created one day after Ikeda's departure. The American press was told that it was established in the "best cooperative spirit" of the Mutual Security Treaty, and it was heralded in the usually anti-American press in Tokyo as symbolic of the "era of new beginnings."[57]

As late as October 1961, the mission of the American delegation on the Trade Committe was unclear. The State Department informed Kennedy that the Committee's "agenda and the specific papers to be discussed are far less important than the fact that the discussions take place."[58] Edwin Reischauer, the American Ambassador to Japan, offered similar praise and advice. A Japanese-speaking Harvard scholar-turned-diplomat, Reischauer thought that the Committee was the best possible expression of the New Pacific Community in the early 1960s. "We have a unique opportunity," he said to the three American members of the Committee in October 1961, "to improve our bilateral relations with Japan and to influence as well the entire course of Japanese domestic and foreign policy."[59]

Maneuvering Japan away from anti-Americanism and into the New Pacific Community would, of course, take time, especially if the only truly active mechanism for American–Japanese cooperation remained a special Trade Committee. George McGovern, Special Assistant to the President, Director of the Food for Peace Program, and a future candidate for President, insisted that the Kennedy administration was up to the task. He saw nothing wrong with "starting small." As one of the few Democrats in Republican South Dakota, McGovern had slowly built a successful political career there. He was used to the slow road to success, and he asked Kennedy not to worry. Winning Japan's favor, he told the President, might begin with the shipment of hundreds of tons of livestock feed to the Japanese island of Hokkaido. The feed shortage there threatened an end to the entire livestock industry in Japan. Since Japan was reluctant to seek American assistance, McGovern recomended the expensive grain shipments in the name of American-Japanese "new beginnings."[60]

Kennedy agreed, and the Trade Committee arranged the mechanics of the grain shipment between late 1961 and March 1962. O. I. Hauge, at Kennedy's Bureau of the Budget, helped to arrange the shipment, but his major concern was textiles, not livestock emergencies. Both industries, he informed the White House, were in a crisis situation. Textiles was the more complicated case. In 1956, Japan supplied 76 per cent of all cotton textile imports to America. By 1962, that percentage had dropped to less than 19 percent. The reason was American tariffs, and the Japanese position in the Trade Committee meetings of 1962 was adamant. They demanded an open share of the market. The Japanese press, and new demonstrations sponsored by Japanese Socialists, supported their trade delegation's argument. Tired of dealing with the sometimes volatile Japanese, Hauge warned Kennedy that the "new beginning" might not be in sight.[61]

Kennedy's answer was a new round of negotiations with the purpose of finding some sort of agreement. That agreement was reached on 1 February 1963, establishing a scaled-down and complicated tariff structure that, from the American view, benefited Japan. The agreement also assisted other Asian nations such as the Republic of China.[62] Hence, international competition did not promise an easy capture of the American market in textiles or other trade items as well.

No one had suggested that the "new beginning" would lead to a quick transition to the happy era of Japanese–American cooperation. Nevertheless, by March 1962, the Kennedy team was already tiring of Japanese complaints and elevating hurdles to achieving the New Pacific Community there. Being on the scene, Ambassador Reischauer faced the brunt of Japanese criticism of American policy. Often viewing matters of policy in a grand, academic approach, Reischauer maintained a minimum interest in the details of trade. War and peace were greater items of interest to him. More sincere on this issue than Kennedy, the Ambassador respected Tokyo's concern over nuclear war and America's nuclear arsenal. In a quiet, gentlemanly style, Reischauer and Ikeda even sparred over the nuclear issue on several occasions.[63]

Reischauer considered Tokyo's negative view towards nuclear weapons as representative of Japan's post-war approach to military matters in general. Since Japan was expected to welcome anti-communist action, including military action, in the New Pacific Community, Reischauer was concerned that Kennedy must frequently address nuclear issues with the Japanese government. He did not consider the implication that Japan's anti-nuclear policy and the New Pacific Community might be incompatible. Instead, it remained another problem of proper maneuvering. Ikeda's protest of Kennedy's early 1962 decision to resume nuclear testing in the atmosphere indicated that that manuevering, as Reischauer cautiously suggested, might be difficult indeed.

> I must express my earnest hope, Mr. President, that you will reconsider your present decision to resume testing. . . . May I hope that before you actually resume your tests you will make a supreme effort to bring about together with the countries concerned an agreement for the suspension of nuclear weapons testing under effective international control and inspection. From what I have expressed in this letter, I trust, Mr. President, that you and the people of your country will show a most serious regard to the feelings of the government and people of Japan.[64]

How to maneuver Japan? The topic was the focus of a State Department-sponsored conference during June 1962. Staff members from the State Department's Policy Planning Division, veteran diplomat W. Averell Harriman, Michael Forrestal and E. J. Thrasher from the White House, and Bill Battle, the newly appointed Ambassador to Australia, met to discuss the future of American–Japanese relations. At the beginning of this secret conference, Harriman admitted that it would be "difficult to keep Japan moving in the direction of democratic processes and an attitude favorable to the West."[65] Japan was "lonely," he said, and still isolated because of the world's memory of the Second World War. Further opening of the American market to the Japanese might weaken the Socialist-led agitation against Washington, Harriman predicted. But, he insisted that unilateral action would be against the best spirit of the New Pacific Community idea. Nations such as Australia and other Pacific powers must open their doors to Japanese products as well.[66]

Ambassador Battle agreed with Harriman's conclusions; however, he correctly observed that the Australian economy was healthy, yet not as sophisticated as the United States. This fact, combined with lingering World War II hatreds against Japan, suggested that the open markets argument would cause political fireworks in Canberra. J. Robert Schaetzel from the State Department, and an architect of the New Pacific Community, pointed out that America must begin a full round of discussions on economic problems with the potential new Pacific Community members in a conference setting. This would break Japanese isolation and coordinate Tokyo's interest in rapid economic development with the interests of other Pacific capitals. As for the specific mechanics of what the New Pacific Community was supposed to do, Schaetzel noted that American–Pacific relations were still too troubled and complex to answer such questions. Given that situation, "it would be a most unfortunate moment to begin even informal [administrative] discussions of the idea."[67]

The June 1962 conference covered the wide range of American–Japanese problems, but only three conclusions were made. The first involved a decision to concentrate on economic contacts, whereby (1) Washington would encourage American industries to welcome Japanese observers, and (2) Japan would be accorded enthusiastic American support in its search for overseas markets. Thirdly, Washington would study the Japanese perception of nuclear-related issues and then vigorously attempt to allay Japanese fears. An American success in these areas would help ease Japan into to the international conference setting that Schaetzel recommended. Nothing remained impossible to the Kennedy team. Japan, they theorized, would be a staunch, happy ally of America and American policy in the Pacific by 1964 and the American general election.[68]

Kennedy welcomed these conclusions, and as early as October 1962, Japanese industrialists and engineers headed for specific American industries to observe and study America's post-war industrial revolution. Eisalsu Sato, the Japanese Minister of International Trade, Sato was an especially welcome guest. Although no trade agreements were reached, Sato was wined and dined by the Kennedys in the grand Camelot style usually reserved for heads of state. Sato, a former Minister of Finance, credited himself for many advances in Japanese economic development. Part of that advancement involved the silencing of communist agitators. Hence, he had the reputation of being one of the Liberal Party's strongest critics of communism as well as radical anti-Americanism. Kennedy appealed to that sentiment, as well as Sato's palate, stressing the anti-communist nature of the coming New Pacific Community.

Sato later thanked Kennedy with the promise that he would persuade Ikeda to be more receptive to American interests in the Pacific. He also praised the New Pacific Community.

The "new wave" of international communism is advancing to the Pacific, as far as the Fiji Islands. To cope with this situation, I feel that it is necessary for the free nations on the Pacific to initiate and develop more effective systems of cooperation and friendship.[69]

Kennedy made headway with the American–Japanese dialogue until the Cuban Missile Crisis of late October 1962. At that time, Kennedy learned that Washington would indeed have to spend as much time on the nuclear issue as on trade matters. The Ikeda government congratulated the Kennedy administration on keeping the peace during the crisis, but it also condemned the President for seriously considering a nuclear strike to resolve it. All of Japan welcomed the peace, yet now demanded strict control of nuclear weapons. The issue transcended party labels, and the Japanese press was particularly disappointed by the turn of events. Having become unusually generous to America in its covering of trade matters, the press returned to its outcry against American military intentions in Asia and elsewhere.[70] The dialogue had soured.

Studying the Japanese approach to nuclear matters, much less politics in general, was a rough assignment. Captain John Roenigk, USN, headed that study team on behalf of the Defense Department. The State Department had thought it more appropriate for a military-related matter to be handled by the military. Hence the problem. Roenigk's study took one year to complete, and it represented one of the American government's first, thoroughly analytical examinations of post-war Japanese politics. The differences between Western political culture and Japanese society were glaring.

As America's naval attaché in Tokyo, Roenigk maintained an obvious interest in naval matters throughout his report. Since his major reader, the President, was an ex-Navy man, that stress was well placed. Japanese opinion against the arrival of American nuclear submarines at Seventh Fleet Headquarters in Yokosuka occupied much of his writing. The Japanese compared those vessels to Commodore Perry's "black ships" of 1853. In short, the Japanese of the 1850s considered Perry the vanguard of an alien, Western culture. Over one hundred years later, America's new "black ships" were the vanguard of a nuclear age that Japan feared. Consequently, opposition to American influences remained virtually unchanged for over a century. Or, at least, Roenigk thought that was the case. He decried the lack of understanding in Washington of Japanese politics, suggesting that the type of diplomatic squabbles that led to Pearl Harbor could be repeated again.[71]

The lengthy Roenigk report was not what the Kennedy administration had expected. It made no specific recommendations to maneuver Japan, but it did dissect the Japanese view of America *vis-à-vis* nuclear issues. Kennedy had to make his own conclusions, and it came two weeks after the submission of the report in the form of a nuclear test ban treaty with the Soviet Union and Britain. This partial ban was Kennedy's response to the dangerous implications of the Cuban Missile Crisis, and he believed that it was the type of response that would also "win Japan to America." "I am confident," Kennedy wrote to Ikeda, "that you will share my deep sense of gratification that this important and encouraging step has been taken. While this is still a heavily armed world, we can all take new hope for a brighter future."[72]

The winning of Japan remained as elusive as ever. On 31 July 1963, one week after Ikeda received Kennedy's message, the Japanese Prime Minister attacked the Kennedy administration for assuming Japanese enthusiasm for the new treaty and for supporting another development, the interest equalization tax. The tax was meant to assault America's balance-of-payments problems, but, to Japan, it promised to affect Tokyo's induction of capital from the United States. This would result in a deficit in Japan's international balance of payments. In general, the pattern of balance of payments between Japan and the United States had undergone significant changes by mid–1963. The trade balance continued to show an excess of imports, while income from special procurements had been on the decrease. On the other hand, payments of royalties on patents and dividends had been rising, aggravating Japan's unfavorable balance in invisible trade. As a result, Japan's balance of payments with the United States between January and July 1963 was $173 million in the red according to Tokyo's foreign exchange statistics.[73]

The interest equalization tax doomed Japan's economic progress, Ikeda complained. Only as an incidental did he comment on the test ban treaty. This was positive news, but it did nothing to address Tokyo's specific opposition to the spreading of America's nuclear arsenal to Japan. It appeared to be only a very minor step in the direction of general nuclear arms control.[74] Thus, Ikeda implied that the Kennedy administration was also afraid to discuss specific matters of policy with the Japanese government.

Indeed, one of the more controversial issues that divided the

United States and Japan was the specific case of the Ryukyu Islands. The issue was of paramount importance in Japanese politics. Kennedy avoided it for obvious reasons. He opposed the "quick" return of the Ryukyus to Japan. But, as long as it remained on the back burner, the Ryukyus issue promised to help keep American–Japanese relations in their difficult condition. It also promised to keep Japan out of the long-in-coming New Pacific Community.

America's national self-interest confused the picture even further. Washington's defense priorities made it most difficult to respond to Japan's nuclear concerns. The realities of domestic economics made it equally as difficult to respond to Tokyo's desire for trade expansion. Caught in the middle was the New Pacific Community and its promise of an American-led Pacific with key, and very content, Pacific nation members.

By the end of his Presidency, Kennedy's new doubt about the 1961 idealism that guided his Pacific policy and other matters also applied to Japan. Shortly before his assassination, he told a group of prefecture-level Japanese politicians that the future of American–Japanese relations was "uncertain." The glowing rhetoric had disappeared.[75] Was America "holding the beachhead" in November 1963? In the Philippines, Kennedy's expensive aid program had effectively demonstrated America's post-war commitment to its former colony. For the time being, America's defense establishment there was secure, and the Filipinos appreciated Kennedy's attention. In Japan, Kennedy could claim that he maintained a more open dialogue with the Japanese government than existed during the Eisenhower years. The defense establishment was also secure, and efforts had been made to answer some Japanese economic complaints.

These accomplishments were not in the realm of the desired grand scheme. The New Pacific Community idea complicated the work of national self-interest, suggesting to the Kennedy team that their practical accomplishments in Japanese and Philippines affairs were never good enough. Moreover, the "holding the beachhead" argument had been overstated. Influenced by Cold War rhetoric and anticommunist domestic politics, the argument implied that a communist takeover, non-alignment, or some political/economic trauma was inevitable in the Philippines and Japan. As Kennedy learned, politics and economics in those two nations were never easy to understand. Neither country faced the imminent disasters that the "beachhead" argument suggested.

Of course, the Kennedy team might have proclaimed the "beachhead" more secure in 1963 than 1961; however, Japanese and Philippines relations were rarely seen in the light of success. Instead, the Kennedy administration expressed clear frustrations over Philippine politics, pleaded ignorance over the Japanese approach to nuclear matters and other issues, and worried about the future of American policy in the Pacific. It was another lesson in the limits of American power, but its implications of arrogance, blind ambition, and interventionist zeal were not apparent to the New Frontiersmen. Enraptured by their own vision, they thought the Pacific was theirs. Only time would determine the success of this charted path to glory.

6 Assumption and "Special Considerations:" the Ryukyus

Of the many problems facing Kennedy's Pacific policy, the Ryukyu Islands offered one of the more intriguing and difficult to New Frontier vision. Ever-conscious of America's image in Asia and always planning to win the Cold War, Kennedy preferred a new status arrangement between the Ryukyus, the United States, and Japan. On the other hand, the Ryukyus in general played a primary role in Pacific defense. Okinawa specifically, and Kadena Air Base especially, represented an important link in that defense. Any Ryukyuan- or Japanese-inspired political deal that even touched upon American defense interests would be unacceptable to the Kennedy administration. The matter created a certain dilemma for the Kennedy team because the large American military presence on Okinawa was a major issue in Tokyo. Could the White House achieve the self-proclaimed noble goals of the New Frontier and maintain the status quo in defense? Could the New Pacific Community truly be built if the Ryukyus issue was not resolved?

Writing in 1966, a renowned Japanese studies specialist, Professor Lawrence Olson, observed that the United States never had any intention of colonizing the Ryukyu Islands. "Despite the visionaries," he concluded, "who saw the island[s] as an entrepôt for Western Pacific trade or even as a Pacific U.N. headquarters – a kind of international Canberra – most responsible Americans had no such fantastic illusions."[1] Olson's "visionaries" were American military officers of the 1950s. Some of them hoped that the treeless, rugged terrain of Okinawa could be "modernized" in an American image, but most of these hopes were confined to Officers' Club discussions and inter-Defense Department memos. Kennedy's vision for Okinawa and the Ryukyus rejected permanent military dominance over local affairs. He inherited a certain reluctance on the part of Washington-based, post-war American officials to begin a Guam-styled military legacy there.[2]

The World War II battle for Okinawa, then a Japanese prefecture and still the most impressive island in the Ryukyu chain, cost nearly 13,000 American lives in 1945. This bloody siege offered the American military a bitter taste of what warfare in Japan proper might be like. Largely thanks to the atomic attacks on Hiroshima and Nagasaki, the projected one million American losses in a Japan invasion were spared. Consequently, Okinawa and its sister islands took on a certain "last stand" heroic image for many Japanese.[3] It also stood as a symbol of the brave American commitment to crush Japanese militarism. World War II ended with these images and symbols clearly in place. During the next several years, President Harry Truman kept American troop strength in the Ryukyus at high and expensive levels. The fear of the resurgence of Japanese militarism was given as the reason for this decision, but it also involved the basic point that America had defeated Japan on the Japanese soil of the Ryukyus.

By the time of the Korean War, justification for the American military occupation of the islands adjusted to the Truman administration's Cold War concerns. Japan was no longer a threat; however, Japan could fall to communism due to pressures from Mao's newly established communist China or from the struggling communist movement within Japan. America's new mission in the Ryukyus was to safeguard Japan and contain communism. Indeed, Okinawa was closer to major Chinese urban centers, such as Shanghai, than to Nagasaki or especially Tokyo. Given the 25-minute flying time between Okinawa and mainland China, Okinawa's position as a forward outpost of the Cold War was assured by the Truman administration.[4]

Okinawa truly demonstrated its military worth as an air base during the Korean War, and the Eisenhower administration dubbed the island "America's unsinkable aircraft carrier."[5] Occupation authorities called it "the Rock." Before World War II, many career officers considered Guam the least desirable assignment. Remoteness, poverty, and typhoons were just a few of the problems that the United States Navy had contended with on Guam, also nicknamed "the Rock." Equally as remote, poor, and in the path of "typhoon alley," Okinawa inherited the honors, while Guam became a civilian-administered Territory of the United States.

In the peace treaty with Japan, the United States acquired complete responsibility for the administration, legislation, and jurisdiction of the Ryukyu Islands. Nearly all of that responsibility, including budgetary matters, stressed Okinawa. The treaty placed the people of the Ryukyus in the position of being residents without a country. They were citizens of neither Japan nor the United States. To prevent any hostility over this arrangement, the Defense Department created the Government of the Ryukyu Islands (GRI). A hybrid version of the advisory, pseudo-legislative Guam Congress of the prewar years, the GRI was organized with legislative, judicial, and executive branches. The Chief Executive of the GRI was appointed by the High Commissioner, the ranking officer of the United States Army. Meanwhile, the 29-member GRI legislature was elected by the people.

Funds for the administration of the islands were provided by the American government acting through the United States Civil Administration of the Ryukyu Islands (USCAR). USCAR "supervised" the GRI, and its ruling body consisted of active duty military officers, as well as retired military men and expatriate civilian Far East "hands." Enjoying a life of power and prestige that might elude them at home, the latter group of USCAR officialdom remained the most energetic and influential in local policy-making.[6]

Following the close of MacArthur's Occupation government in Japan, the people of the Ryukyus began to contemplate their future. Ten years later, when Kennedy came to power, their questions remained unanswered. The islanders enjoyed their own unique culture and language, although the Japanese, over the centuries, had left a permanent imprint on them. Many of them supported the notion to "revert" to Japan, and the reversion issue became a significant one throughout the 1950s. The term Ryukyuan was an American-invented one, implying that the far future of the islands might bring full independence from United States political ties and Japanese cultural connections. But independence and the far future were difficult to perceive for the islanders. Instead, they preferred to debate the mechanics of reversion. The most popular argument in this debate, and for obvious reasons, was the desire to maintain the best of both Japanese and American ties. Originally, this meant complicated political ties to Tokyo, but the economic future of the islands would rest with America.[7]

Evidence of the American post-war economic boom was everywhere, especially on Okinawa. Be it a billboard for "the beer that made Milwaukee famous," the highway from Naha, Okinawa's major urban center, to Kadena Air Base, or the left-hand driving American luxury cars on that highway, it was clear that America had already influenced island life. Kadena, the Third Marine Division, and the army units remained a major island employer. American insurance companies and even automobile dealers had set up operations near the bases. Yet, the islanders remained trapped in a still war-shattered economy. The economic boom was base-related. USCAR rarely diverted funds directly into the local economy, and Washington consented to this neglect. Meanwhile, the Ryukyuans reconstructed Japanese-styled villages and neighborhoods, wondering if the Americans would usurp existing sugar-cane fields for runways or training facilities.[8]

Sugar production was the only significant industry that the islanders could claim to be theirs, and it had not enjoyed success since World War II. First impressions by first-time American visitors to Okinawa and the Ryukyus were based on the growing American military community. Quarters construction for the military and their dependents increased tenfold between 1955 and 1961. Hence, visiting Inspector Generals from the Pentagon and other Americans concluded that the Ryukyuan economy was permanently tied to base development. Moreover, the local base-supporting economy of bars, cheap tailor shops, and crafts grew with Kadena, Torii Station, and other installations.[9]

Despite the American presence, the islanders continued to view themselves as unduly severed from Japan. The Kennedy administration was the first post-war Presidency to consider what this view meant. During the New Pacific Community discussions, it was assumed that the Ryukyuan criticism of both Tokyo's strong-armed dominance of prewar and wartime island life and Washington's "little America" represented a desire for independence. In short, the islander debate over combining Japanese political relations with American economic savvy was labeled an exercise in opportunism. Behind the opportunists' urge, Rusk and Kennedy reasoned, was an independence cause.[10] They were wrong.

Appealing to the independence cause would be difficult, for Kennedy decided that any significant shift in political status would "harm" the security of the bases. Thus, his approach to this region was less flexible than other New Frontier Pacific policies. Considering Okinawa's proven potential in an Asian war, Kennedy had little desire to create security-related problems behind the lines of a Southeast Asian conflict. The nature of these problems was never discussed. Yet once again, he felt that something had to be done. A security-safeguarded reversion would happily throw Ryukyus politics to the Japanese. In the meantime, an American financed and sponsored anti-poverty program for the islands, he believed, would deflate the independence cause. Japan would be a co-sponsor of the efforts. If the Japanese wanted a content Ryukyus, they should contribute heavily to the effort, the Kennedy cabinet concluded. It might build the desired Pacific partnership needed for the New Pacific Community, and it would demonstrate to all Asians that America truly cared about the people of the Ryukyus and their problems.[11] It was yet another plan based on self-proclaimed noble intentions. Contrasts to the years of neglect by Eisenhower and Truman heightened the drama.

But did the plan make any sense? As early as May 1961, the new Kennedy-appointed Assistant Civil Administrator USCAR, Col. W. A. Kelley, said no. Kelley, a former Assistant Secretary of Defense, complained that it was "extremely difficult to satisfy the Ryukyuan people." His complaint involved the fact that the Ryukyuans knew what they did not like, but were at odds over what they favored. Reversion, by its very definition, he pointed out, did not imply a Japanese Ryukyus with American military basing and other privileges. It simply meant a quick return of the islands to Japan. Behind all the local rhetoric, he accurately observed, most islanders preferred centuries-long Japanese ties to the status quo and the potential economic disaster of independence.[12]

Kelley had simple answers to winning the favor of the islanders, safeguarding security, and impressing Asia. He used the same type of Kennedy "cooperative spirit" terminology that permeated New Frontier Pacific policy. The islanders needed to demonstrate to Japan that they wanted to work with Tokyo, not be dominated by them in the prewar/wartime style. America needed to demonstrate its helpful, good intentions in the region. Hence, Kelley recommended the American financing of political elections in the islands beginning in late 1961. Financial assistance to help build Japanese-modelled political parties would be provided as well. All of this would lead, by 1964, to a happy and expanded GRI that did not need USCAR "supervision" or USCAR at all. It would also exercise full power over local affairs and would play the "leading" role in reversion negotiations with Japan and the United States. The propaganda value was immense, and it certainly encouraged a healthy Washington–Naha–Tokyo dialogue.

Kelley's "cooperative spirit" went farther than Kennedy's version. Indeed, the President worried that Kelley's plan moved too fast. He also was not convinced that his administration's belief in Ryukyuan independence ambitions was in error. On the other hand, the issue raised plenty of questions as to how America must exactly proceed. Kennedy ordered the National Security Council to form a special task force to study and recommend a Ryukyus policy by January 1962.[13] In the meantime, he would stand firm on the status quo situation, yet try to avoid the topic with Prime Minister Ikeda.

The Japanese position on the Ryukyus appeared as confusing to the Kennedy administration as the local Ryukyuan debate itself. Capitalizing on Kennedy's "new beginnings" rhetoric, the Japanese Socialist Party clamored in both the *Diet* and in street demonstrations for reversion. Also called the "home islands" issue by the Socialists, the Ryukyus stimulated emotional appeals from the Japanese Left for the "liberation from American occupation." A nation as rich as America, they protested, had not taken the time to eliminate poverty in a few small islands. Consequently, "the home islands" issue not only involved anti-colonial sentiment and Japanese concepts of justice, but also an attack on American competence and intentions.

A fair amount of irony was associated with the Socialist appeal. Over the years, workers from the Ryukyus who sought or found employment on the main islands of Japan were victimized by racist employment regulations and treatment. Popularly viewed as not quite Japanese, not quite American, and generally alien, the Ryukyuans were never defended by the Socialists or the Liberals. In spite of the growing drama of the Ryukyus issue in the early 1960s, Ryukyuan civil rights/civil liberties remained divorced from the political platforms of the major parties. Furthermore, the "home islands" issue also had a certain patriotic ring to it. By mid-1961, Japanese war veterans and the powerful conservative wing of the Liberal Party now urged Ikeda to upstage the Socialists and make some demands on America.[14]

Ikeda agreed with his conservative colleagues, but he planned to avoid specific demands. A fine politician, he permitted the Socialists to align themselves to precise schemes of reversion.[15] This granted him the luxury of attacking those schemes as "impractical" while he discussed the issue with Kennedy. Nevertheless, the matter threatened to remain a serious one in Japanese politics for some time, and the endeavor to upstage the Socialists was always difficult.

Kennedy's confusion on the Japanese view was partially due to the flurry of appeals coming out of Tokyo. Who actually represented a consensus on the issue? Was Ikeda on top of the situation? Kennedy was not sure. Naturally, he combined the information that he received from Reischauer on the Japanese view with the information that he received from USCAR on the local Ryukyus debate. The former was more detailed and voluminous than the latter, and Kennedy often based his perception of all Ryukyus events from what he gathered out of Tokyo and not Naha.[16] But the larger confusion involved Kennedy's mixture of assumptions (independence), security priorities (Okinawa's significance in a Southeast Asia war), and American vision (Pacific partnership and cooperative spirit). Pacific policy was never easy.

At the least, Kennedy was certain that Ikeda was under heavy pressure to win results on reversion. Some positive American response was required to cool Japanese tempers. During the early spring of 1961, Kennedy ordered USCAR to haul down the American flag on all off-base public buildings and hoist the Rising Sun. He also reinstituted the observance of Japanese holidays, and even encouraged patriotic, pro-Japanese parades on those dates. These types of actions were designed for the Japanese and Ryukyuan press in a deliberate effort to influence public opinion before Ikeda arrived for his June 1961 visit to Washington. They were moderately successful.[17]

Although Ikeda wanted it on the agenda, the Ryukyus remained a taboo topic during the state visit. Kennedy's position was clearest in his administration's official and secretly written statement to Ikeda's staff. In that statement, Kennedy promised a special economic aid package for the islands and he urged Ikeda to match it with one of his own. The bases, and their growth, remained American priorities outside of local or Japanese influence. Although this statement read like America's final word, it was meant to be consistent with New Pacific Community ambitions.[18] The Kelley thesis was ignored.

While Kennedy marked time, waiting for the conclusions of Task Force Ryukyus, the Japanese government did not forget the issue, nor did the Socialists. Ikeda continued to believe that America did not understand the significance of Ryukyus reversion to Japanese–American relations. Kennedy hoped it was not as significant as he feared, and he persisted in offering concessions to pro-reversion opinion and Japanese pride. For instance, the All Nippon Airways Company became the first Japanese air carrier to be granted Amer-

ican permission for daily flights to Naha. The announcement was
made with great fanfare, proclaiming that jet age Tokyo–Naha connections would lead to a new era of Japanese–Ryukyuan–American
communication and development.[19]

Yet Ikeda remained curious as to when Kennedy would introduce
specific legislation for the economic development of the Ryukyus.
He also wondered when the formal, personal, and detailed appeal
for Japanese assistance would come. Obviously, this procedure was
a prerequisite to reversion. But when indeed would it come? Finish-
ing its work in December 1961, the Task Force Ryukyus had some
answers for the National Security Council and Kennedy. Ikeda would
have to wait a little longer.

Chaired by White House trouble-shooter, Carl Kaysen, the Task
Force offered the usual decade-long New Frontier formula to success, also recommending clever options to quiet immediate Japanese
concerns. Kaysen's group worked from the basic premise that the
bases posed, as Kennedy had noted, "special consideration" in all
reversion discussions. If Japan and the Ryukyus failed to recognize
those "considerations," then there was nothing Washington could
do.

The Task Force agreed that an economic aid package was
required; however, it suggested only one coordinated and immediate
effort, whereby Japan enjoyed a full financial and administrative
role. Local GRI officials, and particularly GRI critics of American
policy, would be accorded an administrative role equal to Japanese
and American officials. This endeavor would not be considered a
prerequisite to reversion, but part of the reversion process itself.
Once underway, the project would require a formal transfer of local
administrative authority from USCAR to GRI. The project plus the
transfer, the Task Force promised, would take the pressure off
Ikeda. The latter was more to Washington's liking than a Socialist
or ultra-conservative government. If the pressure still continued,
America would "take the offensive" and alter the argument, insisting
on Japanese protection of Ryukyuan civil rights/civil liberties before
proceeding with reversion. This insistence could also be used as a
policy bargaining position whenever Japanese demands "appeared"
to threaten America's basing position.

The threat to security was the focus of the Kennedy policy, but
the actual threat was not discussed until the completion of the Task
Force's work. Quite accurately, the Task Force pointed out that
Japan's worries over the American bases were threefold. First of all,

there was the concern that the growing American military presence meant an imminent war against fellow Asians. Secondly, there was the national humiliation that this war might be largely conducted from still-considered Japanese soil, the scene of Japan's "last stand." And third, there was the fear that America would stockpile nuclear weapons at Kadena. Many Ryukyuans shared these worries, the Task Force noted. Consequently, in the event of war or high diplomatic tensions, Japanese–Ryukyuan protests could lead to violence, the closing of the bases, and the crippling of American military or diplomatic strength. Nevertheless, Ikeda had never implied that the bases must be closed upon final reversion, and the Task Force saw this as an excellent diplomatic opportunity. Indeed, Ikeda would never make such a demand.

Chairman Kaysen had discussed security concerns with Reischauer, Diet Members, and GRI politicians. After months of asking the same questions and receiving similar answers, Kaysen came to the conclusion that greater autonomy for the GRI, the American–Japanese aid scheme, and the promise of Pacific partnership would win Japanese-Ryukyuan respect for the bases. A smooth, decade–long reversion was more than possible. If slowed, a new big money operation would quickly finish the job.

In the global defense network, the Okinawa bases, regardless of their sprawling significance, were inexpensive to the American taxpayer. "Cheap" rents for basing privileges were considered in the realm of ten million dollars per year (Libya) or even $20 to $40 million per year (Morocco). A moderate-to-expensive but fair rent was deemed $150 million per year (Spain). Kaysen recommended the Spanish model with payments made to a Tokyo–Naha consortium until the final reversion agreement was reached. Then, the money would be paid directly to Tokyo. America was paying only $6 million annually in rent to the Ryukyus. In short, it was paying itself a token fee. The new rent would, in a sense, constitute a second aid scheme, for the money would be certainly used for development. It would also deaden independence sentiment as well as impress upon both the islanders and the Japanese government the value America attached to its Okinawa bases. Thus was the promise of big money.

What about Miyako, Ishigaki, Iriomoto and even smaller Ryukyu Islands? The Task Force stressed Okinawa for security reasons, and found that situation both distressing and intriguing. The charges of neglect were strongest outside of Okinawa, and not even the Ikeda government appeared concerned over off-Okinawa events. In the

name of effective image politics, the Task Force recommended a
new Second Task Force to study off-Okinawa problems. In reality,
Kaysen's group had already studied those problems, recommending
a fine balance of economic assistance to each island's needs. But,
the second Force would be a public one designed to illustrate America's active concern in development. It would also provide a forum
for America's Pacific partners' argument, urging full Ryukyuan and
Japanese participation in the interest of the New Pacific
Community.[20]

The Task Force covered all the tenets of the usual New Frontier
approach. Clever and detailed, it still assumed that the islanders
would always harbor independence ambitions, but that American–
Japanese–Ryukyuan cooperation in the post-reversion era would
eventually eliminate those ambitions. It also assumed that Kennedy's
Southeast Asia policy was in danger of a behind-the-lines collapse
at Okinawa if the Ryukyus issue was not adequately addressed. Both
assumptions were exaggerations. The GRI attempted to explain to
the Kennedy administration that independence was not a serious
factor in the story, and that, therefore, America's bases were not in
danger.[21] Nevertheless, the complications of the issue, and particularly its political impact in Tokyo, worried the Kennedy administration, making it difficult for the President to renew his thinking on
independence and potential uprisings against the bases. Kennedy
welcomed the Task Force's plan to eliminate independence sentiment, acomplish reversion, and build the New Pacific Community
by 1972. But it was 1962 that troubled him. Kennedy's tough talk in
mid-1962 about standing firm against alleged Ryukyuan and Japanese
threats to the bases only complicated reversion.[22] It kept the anti-
American implications of the issue alive for Ikeda's critics, making
his government's position a difficult one indeed. And, it did nothing
for Ryukyuan-American relations.

The Task Force represented the American intelligence community's position as well. No further research was conducted by the
CIA or other agencies. Once informed of the Task Force's conclusions, relevant and appropriate to his government, Ikeda wondered why America defined reversion as a decade-long process.
Without question, the Task Force had established a working scenario
for a sooner than ten years success. To Ikeda, as well as the GRI,
success was defined as a matter of months. To Kennedy, reversion
remained a mysterious long-term gamble.[23]

Winning Japan and the Ryukyus to American policy would, it was also assumed, take painstaking patience. But, by April 1962, several of the Task Force's conclusions were already policy. Upon the announcement of new base rent payment intentions, Japanese agreement to the American–Japanese development project, and promises of new obligations for the GRI, Seisaku Ota, Chief Executive of the GRI, informed Kennedy that he was glad to report a significant turn of events. He was offering his first words of praise to the American government. "I have the honor and pleasure to inform you," he wrote, "that the Ryukyu Islands are now on the way to its further development and, in the near future, will achieve so great a prosperity as no one in the past could imagine."[24]

Praise for American policy did not mean its full recognition. Ikeda continued to voice his concern over Washington's intentions for the Okinawa bases and against the slow-moving American reversion schedule. Although largely for domestic consumption, these criticisms promised a rockier road to reversion than the Task Force implied. Meanwhile, Ryukyuan praises were short-lived. In May 1962, over 50,000 Ryukyuans, organized by several GRI politicians and a Ryukyus support group headquartered in Hawaii, sent a petition to Kennedy complaining that the White House was moving too slow on the vital issues facing the islands.[25] Kennedy ignored the complaint.

In terms of practical accomplishments, the Kennedy administration established a $12 million aid program by late 1963, but the precise mechanics of the Japanese and Ryukyuan contribution in this scheme remained lost during endless Washington–Tokyo–Naha discussions. Base renting boosts met a similar fate, and Kennedy was reluctant to place a boosted figure before Congress while the basic dialogue on the Ryukyus remained confused.[26] In its entirety, the issue continued to disturb the larger matters at hand, warm American–Japanese relations and winning the Cold War in the Pacific. Trouble on those fronts helped assure that the New Pacific Community would remain in its elusive state.

With the Ryukyus, Kennedy's New Frontier crossed far over the fine line of complicated goals and ambitions into the realm of assumptions and fears. The facts stood against Ryukyuan independence sentiment and security threats. They indicated Ikeda's desire for quick accommodation on reversion in the interest of rescuing his government from political assault. And they suggested that swiftly answering the charge of economic neglect would lead to Washington's political benefit. Preferring assumptions, perhaps in the name of pleasing Kennedy, Task Force Ryukyus built an expensive scenario that was impossible to achieve. For all effective purposes, the long-term planning, scheming, and policy building of the Kennedy administration subordinated the basic issue, the Ryukyuan desire for reversion and its significance to Japanese politics.

In spite of these difficulties, Kennedy could still claim some success. In the face of Ryukyuan complaints, Japanese protests, and policy-making complications, Kennedy made good his general promise of "new beginnings." His administration recognized the problem of neglect in the Ryukyus and offered a means to resolve it. Kennedy's promise always remained more impressive than his performance, and the "new beginnings" rhetoric never committed the American government to a precise policy of generosity for the Ryukyus or elsewhere. Given even the most modest of follow-up efforts, the politics of promise and "new beginnings" assured limited success to its practitioner. In the case of Kennedy and the Ryukyus, the "new beginnings" led to serious negotiations during the Johnson administration and, as predicted, full reversion by 1972.[27]

More relegated to "new beginnings" rhetoric than other potential members of the New Pacific Community, the Ryukyus certainly symbolized the larger problem of the New Pacific Community itself. Like the Ryukyus policy, the New Pacific Comunity was built on assumptions. Kennedy assumed that specific locations relatively close to the anti-communist front line in Indochina would eventually welcome full American guidance or direction. Although many nations and the American-administered islands welcomed Washington's financial assistance, there was nothing to indicate that local governments would surrender local interests to Kennedy's ambitions.

Kennedy proceeded as if success was inevitable. The facts often stood in opposition to this scheme, and the Ryukyus matter illustrated just how far Kennedy was willing to ignore reality. As long as the reality of Asian/Pacific nationalism and interests remained on the fringes of American policy-making, the New Pacific Community enjoyed little hope of success. Most likely, Kennedy's recognition of that reality would have led to the swift demise of the New Pacific Community vision. He did not entertain such thoughts.

Conclusions

"The essence of the Kennedy legacy," Robert Kennedy once said of his brother, "is a willingness to try and to dare and to change, to hope the uncertain and to risk the unknown."[1] The New Pacific Community reflected this approach to policy; however, its mission always remained beyond the realm of possibility. This specific expression of American ambition died with the President in Dallas.

Speaking about his own approach to policy, Kennedy had declared himself "an idealist without illusions." Hence, Ted Sorensen, Arthur Schlesinger and other close Kennedy associates described the New Frontier as a working manifestation of Kennedy idealism. As a component of the New Frontier, the New Pacific Community better illustrated the border between idealism and the illusions that Kennedy hoped to avoid. Indeed, the New Pacific Community easily crossed over that border, for the successful, single-handed management of the problems of the Pacific was an illusion. Considered both a policy and an idea by the Kennedy team, it represented America's best intentions and best interests. Often standing in contradiction to each other, those intentions and interests led only to confusion and the fear of failure.

Australia, Micronesia, Indonesia, Japan, the Ryukyus, and the Philippines were seen as front lines in the Cold War and rear areas to the Indochina crisis. Each specific location was deemed a special role in winning the Cold War with American guidance, but special problems that might complicate the victory were discovered too late or not at all by the Kennedy team. The very selection of specific Pacific locations for a new American-led organization indicated a certain problem. Good reasons were offered for their inclusion in the New Pacific Community, but plenty of good reasons might have been applied to the Republic of China on Taiwan, the Republic of Korea, or other emerging states.

Although the design of the New Pacific Community might have incorporated the best of reasons by America's "best and brightest," it also set a clear imperial tone. Born out of the early 1961 rallying cry to spread and improve upon American greatness, the New Pacific Community suggested that there was no real alternative to American power in the Pacific. Like the British before them, the Americans reserved the right to demonstrate that power accordingly, "maneuver" governments, and achieve new glories. Henry Fairlie's description of enthusiastic members of the Kennedy era Special Forces and Peace Corps could apply to the architects of the New Pacific Community as well. They "were persuaded," he wrote, "that they could stand on the walls of freedom across the world, enjoying the sensation of empire, exalted by the mission which had fallen to them, but never to bear the pain."[2]

Despite the problems of translating self-proclaimed vision into policy, the Kennedy White House met some success in country-by-country and territory-by-territory relations. Much of that success remained in the area of "new beginnings" politics. Micronesia was placed on the road to "free association" status and the Ryukyus began the "reversion" process. Security interests were assured in the Philippines and Japan, and Indonesia stopped rattling its sword. Meanwhile, there were plenty of warnings that the New Pacific Community might be better relegated to the imagination than American policy. Australia, the projected capital of the new organization, patiently instructed the Kennedy administration on the limits of American power, but the lesson was largely ignored. The Diem assassination resulted in some soul searching in the Oval Office, but there is no evidence to suggest that the New Pacific Community was to be abandoned because of it.

Obviously, in 1963, the New Pacific Community had lost the glitter of 1961. The complications of diplomacy had harmed its progress. On the other hand, it still represented a noble goal, no matter how bizarre and impossible, to the can-do Kennedy team. Remarkably, the financial, administrative, and policymaking mechanics of the organization were never planned or debated. A special atmosphere of sincere cordiality and total commitment to American policy was required on the part of potential members. The Kennedy Cabinet blamed itself for not establishing this foundation. The politics of "maneuvering" was more difficult than they had thought.

Indeed, the very suggestion of the New Pacific Community required a certain arrogance of power. Presidential policy-making within a platform of action and special mission reflected the Kennedy approach. Arthur Schlesinger, Jr, as both historian and New Frontiersman, once wrote that Kennedy associated his administration with those of "heroic," activist presidencies, such as Andrew Jackson and Woodrow Wilson. Testing the Constitutional limits of presidential power appeared to be a criterion for this "heroism," and Schlesinger was cautious in placing his former boss in the ranks of Imperial chief executives. Nevertheless, by setting an Imperial tone in January 1961, Kennedy and his administration won the appropriate label of "Camelot" from a largely adoring press. The label more adequately referred to Kennedy's wealthy, socially polished lifestyle and family than to politics. Yet, there was a second "Camelot," and it referred directly to the arrogant use of power. Even during the Kennedy inaugural, poet Robert Frost implied that through kingly powers the new, young President would champion American greatness throughout the world.

The glory of a next Augustan age
Of a power leading from its strength
    and pride,
Of young ambition eager to be
    tried. . . .

International bullying, couched in the rhetoric of anti-communist rescue and economic goodwill, was nothing new in American Cold War diplomacy. Complete victory in the Cold War was Kennedy's best championed "new idea," and all the "Presidential vigor" and "dynamic leadership" that required, constituted the basic mission of the second "Camelot." The New Pacific Community idea and policy would not have been attempted without this assumption. Ironically, it would be nations that did not support the concept of a powerful chief executive, such as Australia, or countries that were more than aware of the powers of the national leader, such as Indonesia, which troubled the progress of Kennedy's New Pacific Community. Despite the alleged good intention of destroying the abrasive "ugly American" image in the Asian/Pacific Third World and elsewhere, the Kennedy team planned to replace it with a more cleverly designed package of arrogance. National self-interest, which included the Cold War victory, implied brilliant maneuvering tactics throughout the Third World, "massive retaliation," and a new spirit of anti-communist, messianic diplomacy. The New Pacific Community always symbolized this Kennedy-described, modern and proper direction in American foreign policy.

Assuming that America had won an unassailable position as a Great Power during the Second World War, Kennedy approached foreign policy-making from the point of view that Truman and Eisenhower had not taken full advantage of that status while producing the Truman and Eisenhower Doctrines. In spite of the suggestion that he would succeed where his predecessors had failed, Kennedy still offered the impression to Khrushchev and others that his desire to see America loved in the Third World as well as victorious in the Cold War constituted a confusion in purpose. To Khrushchev, Kennedy's talk of peace, development, and Cold War confrontation represented a foreign policy rife with contradictions. This approach to policy reflected Kennedy's youth and inexperience, Khrushchev theorized, tempting the Soviet Premier to test his theory in Berlin, Laos, and Cuba. The near nuclear disaster during the Cuban Missile crisis proved Khrushchev especially wrong and forced Kennedy to reconsider the possible price of Cold War victory. Rhetoric and mission aside, it was largely in this area of nuclear crisis that separated, for all practical purposes, the Kennedy administration from its predecessors. Indeed, many observers suggested that it was Kennedy's "pay any price, bear any burden" inaugural promise that eventually encouraged the Cuban Missile crisis of October 1962.

In the Third World, "pay any price, bear any burden" included Special Forces, Peace Corps activists, and a certain flamboyant style to policy-making. The effort to transcend this approach with even more "vigorous" endeavors, such as the New Pacific Community, met as little success as the former. In spite of the shifts in tactics, American policy in the Third World remained essentially unchanged during the early 1960s. Third World economic assistance packages were generously concocted during the Kennedy years in contrast to the more balanced budget-conscious Eisenhower period, but American influence in the Third World remained as questionable as ever. Kennedy's foreign policy-making contrasts to Eisenhower remained most obvious in the realm of promise and vision.

Playing an important part within the Kennedy promise and vision of Cold War victory, Vietnam especially tested the limits of American power. The young President answered the test with an escalated US military presence. His discomfort with this decision has led a variety of authors and Kennedy family members to comment on the possibilities of a Kennedy-ordered withdrawal from Vietnam during the period of the 1964 election. Nevertheless, the abandonment of the Saigon regime had not been part of the Kennedy foreign policy. Presidents Johnson and Nixon continued the military commitment, demonstrating the bipartisan continuity of anti-communism. Theories and policies of coexistence and *détente* with communism grew with America's casualty figures in Southeast Asia, but Kennedy's successors did not reject the role of champion of Free World causes.

The tragedy of military defeat in Vietnam, and the associated traumas of social unrest at home, forced Johnson and Nixon to consider the limits of American power in a much more dramatic light than Kennedy. Yet, this new reflection did not mean that Kennedy's dream of Cold War victory was forgotten. While conservative Republicans, such as Ronald Reagan, associated that victory with "patriotic" foreign policy, moderate/liberal Democrats, such as Clement Zablocki, Chairman of the House of Representatives Foreign Affairs Committee during the 1970s and early 1980s, insisted that Congress be considered in all presidential foreign policies of "vision" in the future.

Zablocki's argument, better known as the War Powers Act, established a strict adherence to Constitutional checks and balances *vis-à-vis* presidential decisions involving armed interventionism. A major goal of the Act included a deliberate Congressional attack, supported by majority public opinion, against the so-called Imperial Presidency. Establishing the precedent of Presidential-Congressional cooperation in the effort to prevent "future Vietnams," the War Powers Act suggested to those who were nostalgic for the vigorous and visionary leadership of the New Frontier that the good old days might never return. Indeed, given the unhappy memory of Vietnam, the specter of World War III during the Cuban Missile crisis, the military alert over Berlin, and the Bay of Pigs invasion of Cuba, the first "Camelot" has remained more appealing than the second in popular memory. Hence, Kennedy's endeavors with the New Pacific Community are often overlooked in the scholarly and journalistic community.

Kennedy's policy for the entire Asian/Pacific region had been simply stated. Furthering the anti-communist cause, never shrinking from the use of military force within that cause, downplaying the "ugly American" image, and shoring-up defense arrangements were its major elements. The latter two elements were particularly important to the New Pacific Community, while the more militant expressions of the Kennedy policy were reserved for Indochina. For all practical purposes, the New Pacific Community illustrated a new dilemma in post-war American policy, the marriage of extremely difficult, if not impossible, goals to diplomacy. This procedure confused the very policy-makers who created it, often stimulating strained relationships with the nations and territories that they hoped to influence. It was an exercise in American arrogance, and it met few successes.

Notes and References

1 Finding the "Right Key:" Kennedy and the New Pacific Community

1. William J. Lederer and Eugene Burdick, *The Ugly American* (New York, 1960), pp. 163, 233.
2. "The United States and Our Future in Asia," Excerpts from the Remarks of Senator John F. Kennedy (Hawaii, 1958), JFK Library, Senate Files.
3. Ibid. Championing America's virtue and image abroad, as well as American self-interest, always remained a difficult task for Kennedy. See Ronald Nurse, "America Must Not Sleep: The Development of John F. Kennedy's Foreign Policy Attitudes, 1947–1960" (Ph.D. dissertation: Michigan State University, 1971), James Dorsey, "Vietnam 'a can of snakes,' Galbraith told JFK," *Boston Globe* (28 January 1974), Stephen Pelz, "John F. Kennedy's 1961 Vietnam War Decisions," *Journal of Strategic Studies* (December 1981), Ian McDonald, "Kennedy Files Show President's Dismay at CIA Power," *The Times* (London, 2 August 1971), JFK Library, Excerpts from Biographical Files.
4. Secretary of State Dean Rusk to Kennedy, 2 February 1961, and "The New Pacific" (Speech in Hawaii, August 1960), JFK Library, POF/Box 111 and Senate Files.
5. John F. Kennedy, *Public Papers of the President, 1961*) (Washington, D.C., 1961), pp. 174–5. These comments were made during the President's push to create the "Alliance for Progress" program for the Latin American/Caribbean states.
6. Kennedy, *Public Papers of the President, 1961*, p. 399.
7. Ibid., *1963*, p. 652.
8. Kennedy's early cabinet meetings on foreign affairs topics often became energetic discussions on how to win the Cold War. A winning strategy, whether in allied favor or not, was acceptable. This type of approach is skillfully noted in Roger Hilsman, *To Move a Nation: The Politics of Foreign Policy in the Administration of John F. Kennedy* (New York, 1967), pp. 541–76, and Herbert Parmet, *Jack: The Struggles of John F. Kennedy* (New York, 1980), pp. 399–416. Other authors have attempted to separate the Kennedy record from the Kennedy promise, concluding that Americans have created a Kennedy patriotic myth since the November 1963 assassination. Lewis Paper, *The Promise and the Performance: The Leadership of John F. Kennedy* (New York, 1975), Henry Fairlie, *The Kennedy Promise: The Politics of Expectation* (New York, 1972), William Leuctenburg, *In the Shadow of FDR: From Harry Truman to Ronald Reagan* (Ithaca, 1983). More specific studies of Kennedy's foreign policy, particularly stressing the Third World, have drawn distinctions between New Frontier foreign policy promises and have

116

found them wanting. Richard D. Mahoney, *JFK: Ordeal in Africa* (New York, 1983), Montague Kern, Patricia Levering, Ralph Levering, *The Kennedy Crises: The Press, the Presidency, and Foreign Policy* (Chapel Hill, 1983).

9. Richard Walton, *Cold War and Counterrevolution: The Foreign Policy of John F. Kennedy* (New York, 1972), pp. 202–34.

10. See the conclusion to Theodore C. Sorensen, *Decision-Making in the White House* (New York, 1964).

11. For a fine "Socratic" analysis of Kennedy's Vietnam cabinet decisions, see William Rust, *Kennedy in Vietnam* (New York, 1985), pp. ix-xvii.

12. Kennedy's preference for keen analysis of foreign policy options, and his self-appointed role as America's Number 1 intellectual diplomat, is praised in Arthur M. Schlesinger, Jr, *A Thousand Days: John F. Kennedy in the White House* (Boston, 1965), pp. 406–47.

13. "Observations on Proposal for a New Pacific Community and Review of April Cabinet Sessions," J. Robert Schaetzel to George Ball, internal State Department memorandum and report, 2 November 1961, JFK Library, NSF/Box 345. This extensive year-end account, declassified in the early 1980s, is the basis for the succeeding notes.

14. Ibid.

15. Ibid.

16. Ibid.

17. Ibid. See also my "The Promise Fulfilled: John F. Kennedy and the New Frontier in Guam and the Trust Territory of the Pacific Islands, 1961–1963," Alexj Ugrinsky (ed.), *JFK* (Westport, CT, 1985).

18. Schaetzel to Ball, 2 November 1961, and Kennedy to Secretary of Defense Robert McNamara, 31 January and 1 February 1961, JFK Library, NSF/Box 345 and Guam/Box 101. Anthony Solomon, Chairman of the US Survey Mission to Guam and the Trust Territory, to Kennedy, plus Survey Report, 9 October 1963, Pacific Collection (Confidential File), Micronesian Area Research Center, University of Guam (hereafter referred to as MARC).

19. Schlesinger, *A Thousand Days*, p. 532; Kennedy to Sukarno, 9 December 1961 and Schaetzel to Ball, 2 November 1961, JFK Library, POF/Box 111 and NSF/Box 345.

20. Ibid. (last citation). Kennedy believed that tough "crisis management" decisions were always possible. Indeed, a President must embrace conflicts with a certain "masculine will" and resolve them with "vigor." Kennedy's efforts to demonstrate his masculinity via tough decisions is examined in Garry Wills, *The Kennedy Imprisonment: A Meditation on Power* (Boston, 1982), pp. 141–50, 165–74, 176–87, 219–31. Other authors see Kennedy's drive to "influence world history" and leave a "lasting legacy" as representative of what Arthur Schlesinger, a former member of the Kennedy team, called "the Imperial Presidency." Consequently, national security problems were always examined by Kennedy in an intensely "personal" fashion within his "cult of authority," the cabinet. Theodore J. Lowi, *The Personal President: Power Invested, Promised Unfulfilled* (Ithaca, 1985), and David Burner and Thomas

R. West, *The Torch is Passed: The Kennedy Brothers and American Liberalism* (New York, 1984), p. 212.

21. Schaetzel to Ball, 2 November 1961, and Cabinet discussion and memorandum on the visit of the Australian Prime Minister, Robert Menzies, to the White House, 23 February 1961, JFK Library, NSF/Box 345 and POF/Box 111.

22. The point of "importance" is dramatically illustrated in Kennedy's correspondence to Prime Minister Hayato Ikeda of Japan during the Cuban Missile Crisis. Kennedy noted that, regardless of the outcome of the Crisis, the United States would maintain its commitments to Japan and the Pacific. Praising the progress of US–Japanese and US–Pacific relations in general, he also promised a "vigorous" reaffirmation of America's peaceful goals in the Pacific region once the Crisis was over. Nothing would disturb America's interests in the Pacific, he said. Kennedy to Ikeda, 22 October 1962, JFK Library, POF/Box 120.

2 Rust Removal: the New Frontier in Guam and the Trust Territory of the Pacific Islands

1. Several historical works exist on individual western Pacific islands and their development and security problems; however, there is no specific study concerning the evolution of Washington's policy towards modern Micronesia, particularly during the pivotal Kennedy era. The most successful political/strategic studies of selected islands in the region remain Daniel T. Hughes and Sherwood G. Lingenfelter, *Political Development in Micronesia* (Columbus, 1974), pp. 3–309; James H. Webb, Jr, *Micronesia and U.S. Pacific Strategy: A Blueprint for the 1980s* (New York, 1974), pp. 61–102; and David Nevin, *The American Touch in Micronesia* (New York, 1977), pp. 70–96.

2. For Nucker's comments and a brief account of 1950s Micronesia, see: E. J. Kahn, Jr, *A Reporter in Micronesia* (New York, 1966) p. 119. Following this episode, Nucker resigned and was replaced by his assistant, M. W. Goding, a Democrat sympathetic to the Kennedy administration.

3. J. Robert Schaetzel to George Ball: Memorandum on Proposal for a New Pacific Community, 2 November 1961, JFK Library NSF/Box 345.

4. Ralph Dungan, Special Assistant to the President, to Bradford Smith, 20 April 1961, JFK Library, White House Central Files/Box 940.

5. Jose Benitez, Deputy High Commissioner of the Trust Territory, to JFK, 23 June 1961 and JFK to Benitez, 20 July 1961, ibid.

6. Aspinall to Kennedy, 20 March 1962, JFK Library, White House Central Files/ Box 940. "Micronesia is a term which is often misused and misunderstood. Generally, the term is used synonymously with the Trust Territory of the Pacific Islands; this is a political description. Geographically, Micronesia includes the Marianas, Carolines, Marshalls, Kiribati (Gilberts), and Nauru." Dirk Ballendorf, Director, Micronesian Area Research Center (MARC), University of Guam. This work uses "Micronesia" in a geographic sense.

7. JFK to Tupua Tamasese Mea'ole, Malietoa Tanumafili II, Head of State, Western Samoa, December 27, 1961, JFK Library, POF/Box 123a.

8. "The United States and Hawaii and Our Future in Asia," JFK Library, Excerpts from the Remarks of Senator John F. Kennedy, 1958.

9. Kennedy to his parents, 12 September 1943, JFK Library, Personal Papers of JFK.

10. John Kennedy, *Profiles in Courage* (New York, 1956).

11. JFK to M. W. Goding, High Commissioner of the Trust Territory, 3 July 1962 and White House Press Release: "Guam and Executive Order 8683," 23 August 1962, JFK Library, White House Central Files/Box 572 and Guam/Box 101.

12. T. J. Reardon, Special Assistant to the President, to John Hosmer, 28 December 1962, JFK Library, White House Central Files/Box 940.

13. Benitez to Ted Sorensen, Special Advisor to the President, 9 November 1962, and "Statement by the President: Guam and the Trust Territory of the Pacific Islands," 23 August 1962, JFK Library, White House Central Files/Box 940 and POF/Box 77.

14. For background on this period, see Timothy P. Maga, "The Citizenship Movement in Guam, 1946–1950," *Pacific Historical Review*, Vol. 53 (February 1984), pp. 59–77; Earl S. Pomeroy, *Pacific Outpost: American Strategy in Guam and Micronesia* (Stanford, 1951), pp. 161–80.

15. For background see the introductory material to Dr Anthony Solomon to Kennedy, 9 October 1963: "Report by the U.S. Government Survey Mission to the Trust Territory of the Pacific Islands," MARC, Pacific Confidential Collections.

16. Memorandum for David Bell, Director, Bureau of the Budget, 2 March 1961, and Ralph Dungan, Special Assistant to the President, to A. B. Won Pat, Speaker, Guam Legislature, 9 October 1961, JFK Library, White House Central Files/Box 940.

17. Dungan to R. J. Bordallo, Chairman, Democratic-Popular Party of Guam, 16 August 1961, JFK Library, White House Central Files/Box 825.

18. Flores to Kennedy, 21 January 1961, JFK Library, Guam/Box 101.

19. Kennedy to McNamara, 31 January–1 February 1961, ibid.

20. Ibid.

21. Senator Oren Long to Lawrence O'Brien, Special Assistant to the President, and special report, 2 February 1961, JFK Library, White House Central Files/Box 940.

22. Ibid. Benitez to Lawrence O'Brien, Special Assistant to the President, 13 July 1961, JFK Library, White House Central Files/Box 940.

23. Ibid. Kennedy to Flores, 8 February 1961, JFK Library, Guam/Box 4101.

24. Petition from the Sixth Guam Legislature, February 1961, JFK Library, White House Central Files/Box 940.

25. Assistant Secretary of the Interior John Carver to Kennedy and text of Daniel Speech, 20 May 1961, ibid.

26. This is a major theme of Alain C. Enthoven and K. Wayne Smith, *How*

Much is Enough? Shaping the Defense Program, 1961–1969 (New York, 1971).

27. Kennedy to Benitez, 20 July 1961, JFK Library, White House Central Files/Box 940.

28. Sampson to Kennedy and CENTPAC/WESTPAC report, May 1961, JFK Library, POF/Box 77.

29. Dungan to Won Pat, 9 October 1961, JFK Library, ST51–1/Box 940.

30. *Micronesian Reporter*, Vol. x (March-April 1962), 1–23, MARC.

31. Reports to the Secretary of State, 25 January–16 February 1962, JFK Library, POF/Box 1236.

32. Ibid. For background on NTTU, see Mike Malone, "The CIA in Micronesia," *Glimpses of Micronesia*, Vol. 23 (1983), pp. 28–30; Bob Woodward, "CIA Bugging Micronesia Negotiations," *The Washington Post* 12 December 1976), p. 1.

33. O'Brien to Aspinall, 20 March 1962, and Aspinall to O'Brien, 21 March 1962, JFK Library, White House Central Files/Box 940.

34. Manuel F. L. Guerrero, Acting Governor of Guam, to JFK, 26 February 1963, and JFK to Guerrero, 6 March 1963, JFK Library, White House Central Files/Box 940 and 572.

35. Governor Daniel to Udall, Connally to Kennedy and Udall, and Udall to Connally, 9 December 1961 and 3 January 1962, JFK Library, White House Central Files/Box 940.

36. Captain Sampson to David Bell, 20 April 1962, Kennedy to Governor Daniel, 30 April 1962 and 14 May 1962, Captain Robert J. Oliver, Assistant Chief of Naval Operations, to Kennedy, 16 May 1962, ibid.

37. Kennedy to M. Wilfred Goding, High Commissioner of the Trust Territory of the Pacific Islands, 3 July 1962, Norman Paul, Assistant Secretary of Defense, to Senator Clair Engle, 19 September 1962, McGeorge Bundy, Department of State, to Dean Knowles Ryerson, 4 December 1962, ibid.

38. Ibid. (last entry). Otis Beasley, Assistant Secretary of the Interior, to David Bell, Director, Bureau of the Budget, 26 February 1962, JFK Library, White House Central Files/Box L940.

39. Dellinger to JFK, 27 August 1962, and White House "Report on the Economic and Social Status of Guam and the Trust Territory of the Pacific Islands," August 1962, ibid.

40. "Trust Territory Receiving World-Wide Publicity," *Micronesian Reporter*, Vol. X (March-April 1962), p. 16, JFK Library, Guam/Box 101.

41. Strik Yoma, "A Matter of Ideals" (an open letter to the Kennedy administration), ibid., p. 20.

42. Kennedy to Guerrero, 6 March 1963 (inauguration), JFK Library, White House Central Files/Box 572.

43. See the annual reports of the Deputy High Commissioner of the Trust Territory of the Pacific Islands, Jose Benitez, 1962, 1963. Benitez was an enthusiastic admirer of Kennedy, and his reports were especially prepared for the President, ibid.

44. Ibid.

45. National Security Action Memorandum No. 243, 9 May 1963, National

Archives, Record Group 273, Records of the National Security Council, File NWFJ.
46. Solomon to JFK, 9 October 1963 and "Report by the U.S. Government Survey Mission to the Trust Territory of the Pacific Islands," MARC, Pacific Confidential Collections.
47. Ibid.
48. Ibid.
49. Ibid.
50. Ibid. JFK to Udall, 4 November 1963, JFK Library, White House Central Files/Box 940.
51. United Nations General Assembly: "Report on the Situation with Regard to the Implementation of the Declaration on the Granting of Independence to Colonial Countries and Peoples," 17 December 1962, John Hosmer to Acting Secretary General U Thant, UN, 13 November 1962 and Richard Maguire to Hosmer, 20 December 1962, ibid., Solomon Report, MARC, Pacific Confidential Collections.
52. Ibid. (last entry). Kennedy to Solomon and Udall, 4 November 1963, JFK Library, White House Central Files/Box 940.
53. United Nations General Assembly, *Report on Micronesia, 1964*, pp. 38–39.
54. Kennedy to Udall, 4 November 1963, JFK Library, White House Central Files/Box 940.
55. Solomon Report, MARC, Pacific Confidential Collections.
56. National Security Council to Kennedy, 14 June 1963, State Department Memorandum for McGeorge Bundy, 14 June 1963, Kenneth O'Donnell, Special Assistant to the President, to Ed Engledow, Special Assistant to the Governor of Guam, October 25, 1963, JFK Library, White House Central Files/Box 940.
57. "Events leading to the formation of the Office of Micronesian Status Negotiations," Report of the Subcommittee on Asian/Pacific Affairs, House of Representatives, to author, July 1985 (personal file).

3 Friend or Foe? Australia and Destiny

1. Rusk to Kennedy, 2 February 1961, JFK Library, POF/Box 111.
2. Ibid.
3. Ibid.
4. National Security Council (NSC) Briefing Papers for Kennedy–Menzies Meeting, 22 February 1961: "U.S.–Australian Relations," "International Organizations" and "China," ibid.
5. Richard L. Sneider, Officer in Charge – Japanese Affairs, State Department to Kennedy, 23 June 1961: Memorandum on "Ikeda and China," and Garcia to Kennedy, 24 May 1961, JFK Library, White House Central File/Box 62 and POF/Box 123a.
6. NSC Briefing Papers – "China," JFK Library, POF/Box 111.
7. State Department Memorandum: Current Status of U.S.–Australian Relations, 14 March 1962, ibid.
8. Briefing Material, West New Guinea and Indonesia, Rusk to Kennedy,

23 February 1961, ibid. For background on the New Guinea issue, one of the most analytical accounts remains H. S. Albinski, "Australia and the Dutch New Guinea Dispute," *International Journal* (Autumn 1961), pp. 358–62.

9. Cabinet discussion and memorandum on Prime Minister Menzies' visit, 23 February 1961, and Year End Observations on Proposal for the New Pacific Community, J. Robert Schaetzel, State Department, to Under Secretary of State George Ball, 2 November 1961, JFK Library, POF/Box 111 and NSF/Box 345.

10. Briefing Material (Menzies' visit), February 23 1961, JFK Library, POF/Box 111.

11. The struggle to maintain Australian "identity" in the face of America's "world interests" is a major focus of Trevor Reese, *Australia, New Zealand, and the United States, 1941–68* (London, 1969). State Department memorandum: "Status and Atmosphere of U.S.–Australian Relations," February 23 1961, JFK Library, POF/Box 111.

12. Ibid.

13. "Background on Prime Minister Menzies," Howard Beale, Australian Ambassador to the United States, to Rusk, 23 February 1961, ibid.

14. Prime Minister Menzies' visit, February 1961, ibid. Although declassified in 1978, the Kennedy-Menzies discussions were not easily accessible to historians until 1984. Kennedy followed the State Department's recommended policy positions to the letter.

15. Ibid.

16. Ibid. Kennedy once noted that Laos was "a symbolic test of strengths between the major powers of the West and the Communist bloc." He perceived American weakness there as not only requiring stronger policies in Vietnam, but a tightening of anti-communist missions around the world. The Senator Gravel Edition, *The Pentagon Papers: The Defense Department History of United States Decision-making on Vietnam* (Boston, 1971), Vol. *II*, pp. 22, 33, 48–49.

17. J. Wilcynski, "Australia's Trade With China," *India Quarterly* (April-June 1965), pp. 154–167; State Department memorandum: "Communist China and Australia," Februuary 23, 1961, and Prime Minister Menzies' visit, February 1961, JFK Library, POF/Box 111; Harry G. Gelber, *Australia, Britain and the EEC, 1961–1963* (Melbourne, 1966), p. 47.

18. The inability, or refusal, of the Kennedy administration to understand the Cold War positions of so-called "little states" is noted in Gabriel Kolko, *Anatomy of a War: Vietnam, The United States, and the Modern Historical Experience* (New York, 1985), p. 112.

19. US–Australian Relations; Australia's Internal Political Situation, State Department memo to Kennedy, March 13 1962, JFK Library, POF/Box 111; D. W. Rawson, "Foreign Policy and Australian Parties," *World Review* (July 1962), pp. 16–23.

20. Intelligence Despatch, US Embassy – Canberra, to Ball, "Australian Character, Psychology and Attitudes" (summary of March-June 1962 correspondence to Ball), and US–Australian Relations/Australia's Internal Political Situation, State Department memo to Kennedy, March 13 1962, JFK Library, NSF/Boxes 6–8 and POF/Box 111.

21. Ibid. (all of previous note).
22. Ibid.
23. Briefing notes, Kennedy–Menzies meeting, and press conference comments, June 20 1962, JFK Library, NSF/Boxes 6–8; Reese, *Australia, New Zealand, and the United States*, pp. 303–4.
24. See the following chapter for the policy details.
25. Kennedy–Menzies meeting, June 20 1962, State Department memo on Australian Labor Party and Foreign Affairs, June 18 1962, and Visits of Australian Labor Party Representatives, July 5–10 1962; William Battle, US Ambassador to Australia, to Rusk, 15 June and July 20 1962, JFK Library, NSF/Boxes 6–8.
26. The suggestion of establishing and maintaining only one small base dated to April 1962 and was made by Kennedy's military advisors. It came up during a request, offered by the US Air Force, that the Menzies government permit high altitude air sampling operations by American planes from Australian airfields. The project, code named Clear Sky (Crow Flight), was quickly overshadowed by the navy base issue. For details on both matters, see: Rusk to Joint Chiefs of Staff, April 10 1962, US Embassy–Canberra to Rusk, May 16 and June 5 1962, Speech by Prime Minister Menzies on North West Cape, May 17 1962, Ball to Battle, July 23 1962, and Battle to Rusk, March 25 1963, ibid.
27. Ralph Dungan, White House Staff, to Kennedy, May 14 1962, "Our Ties With U.S. Close," *The Herald* (January 12 1963), p. 11; Memo on press attacks and Labor party, Battle to Rusk, March 8 1963, ibid.
28. Ibid. (all of above notes); White House Press Release on President's intention to appoint William C. Battle as Ambassador to Australia, May 25 1962, JFK Library, POF/Box 111.
29. State Department memos on the Labor party and its impact on Australian foreign affairs, July 19 and 20 1963, Kennedy to Menzies, August 19 1963, Michael Forrestal, National Security Council, to McGeorge Bundy, White House, October 15 1963, Briefing notes and Kennedy–Barwick meeting, October 17 1963, JFK Library, NSF/Boxes 6–8.
30. Kennedy–Barwick meeting, ibid.
31. State Department memo: Status of US-Australian relations, November 1963, ibid. Current scholarship on the Diem coup places greater blame on Kennedy than ever before, but also examines the significance of Kennedy's personal disgust for the event. See Rust: *Kennedy in Vietnam*. The importance of family, honor, and commitment was a legacy left by Joseph P. Kennedy to his children. The relevance of that legacy to policy-making is noted in Edward M. Kennedy (ed.), *The Fruitful Bough: A Tribute to Joseph P. Kennedy* (private publication, 1966), JFK Library.

4 New Frontier v. Guided Democracy: Kennedy, Sukarno, and Indonesia

1. Schlesinger, *A Thousand Days*, p. 532.
2. Kennedy to Sukarno, 9 December 1961, JFK Library, POF/Box 111.

3. National Security Memorandum No. 179, 16 August 1962, JFK Library, NSF/Box 338.
4. Ibid. Sukarno's career has been well-examined by researchers. Some of the best analytical works in English remain older texts, such as: Hal Kosut (ed.), *Indonesia: The Sukarno Years* (New York, 1970), Cindy Adams, *Sukarno* (Indianapolis, 1965), General Abdul H. Nasution, *The Indonesian National Army* (Djakarta, 1956), Sheldon W. Simon, *Broken Triangle: Peking, Djakarta, and the PKI* (Baltimore, 1969), and David Denoon, "Indonesia: Transition to Stability?," *Current History*, Vol. 61 (December 1971), pp. 332–338.
5. Ibid. Howard Jones, a keen observer of Indonesian developments and the US Ambassador to Indonesia during the Kennedy years, offers a fine American portrait of Indonesian politics. Convinced that JFK's New Frontier promised lasting peace for the Pacific as well as years of warm Indonesian relations, Jones's account of Sukarno and American policy remains invaluable to the serious student and scholar. Howard P. Jones, *Indonesia: The Possible Dream* (New York, 1971).
6. Cabinet Discussion of National Security Memorandum No. 179: US Policy Toward Indonesia, 16 August 1962, JFK Library, POF/Box 119.
7. Ibid.
8. Ibid.
9. Briefing Material to Sukarno Meeting, April 1961, and "Background to Plan of Action for Indonesia," Department of State, 2 October 1962, JFK Library, NSF/Box 338.
10. Ibid.
11. For Cabinet summary opinion and the Peace Corps role, see ibid., and National Security Memorandum 179; Wills, *The Kennedy Imprisonment*, introduction; Theodore C. Sorensen, *The Kennedy Legacy* (New York, 1969), pp. 15–20.
12. Cabinet discussion and memorandum on Australian Prime Minister Robert Menzies visit to the US, 23 February 1961, and Year End Observations on Proposal for the New Pacific Community, Rusk to Kennedy, 2 November 1961, JFK Library, POF/Box 111, and NSF/Box 345.
13. Ibid. Rusk to Kennedy, 26 October 1962; Jones, *Indonesia*, pp. 194–5, 198, 280.
14. Kennedy–Sukarno meeting summary points, JFK Library, April 1961, POF/Box 111. Kennedy's comments against US meddling in Third World affairs was largely influenced by the Bay of Pigs crisis which coincided with Sukarno's arrival. Cuba was never mentioned in the Kennedy–Sukarno meeting.
15. Sukarno to Kennedy, 16 December 1961, JFK Library, POF/Box 110.
16. State Department internal memorandum and report: "The Soviet Union and the Newly Emerging Forces," 11 January 1963 JFK Library, NSF/Box 115; State Department, *The Sino-Soviet Economic Offensive Through June 30, 1962*, Unclassified Research Memorandum RSB–145, 18 September 1962.
17. Quoted in Herbert Feith, "Soviet Aid to Indonesia," *Nation* (New South

Wales, Australia), 3 November 1962, p. 11. Dr Feith was the Australian government's foremost expert in Indonesian affairs.
18. "The National-Liberation Movement at the Present Stage," *Kommunist* (September 1962), translated as the lead article in *The Current Digest of the Soviet Press*, 7 November 1962.
19. Text of Khrushchev's speech appears in *The New York Times*, 12 February 1960, p. 4.
20. State Department memo/report ("Emerging Forces"), 11 January 1963, JFK Library, NSF/Box 115.
21. Ibid.
22. State Department internal memorandum and report: "Indonesia – An Aspirant Great Power?," 11 January 1963, JFK Library, NSF/Box 115; Embassy of Indonesia, *PIA News Bulletin*, 8 October 1962, p. 1, Section A.
23. Ibid. (all of preceding note), and *PIA News Bulletin*, 5 October 1962, p. 5, Section B; "Indonesia's Armoury," *Far Eastern Economic Review* (Hong Kong), 1 November 1962, p. 283.
24. The Philippines position is noted throughout the sources cited in Notes 22 and 23.
25. For Kennedy's New Frontier relations with the Philippines, see the succeeding chapter.
26. State Department memo/report "Aspirant Power?," 11 January 1963, JFK Library, NSF/Box 115.
27. Ibid.
28. Ibid.
29. *PIA News Bulletin*, 18 February 1960, p. 3, Section A.
30. Ibid., 23 October 1962, p. 1, Section B.
31. State Department memo/report "Aspirant Power?", 11 January 1963, JFK Library, NSF/Box 115.
32. McGeorge Bundy to the President, 26 July 1962 and Robert Kennedy to the President, 16 August 1962, JFK Library, NSF/Box 338; Arthur M. Schlesinger, Jr, *Robert Kennedy and His Times* (New York, 1978), pp. 612, 614–616.
33. Briefing Material to Sukarno Meeting – Pope Case, February 1961, Secretary of the Army Stahr to Kennedy, 30 March 1961, Ambassador Jones to Kennedy, 14 February 1962, Jones to Rusk, 15 February 1962, General Council, Central Intelligence Agency, to Kennedy, 12 July 1962, Pope to Kennedy, 11 July 1962, JFK Library, POF and NSF/Boxes 119 and 338.
34. Rusk to Jones, 26 October 1962, JFK Library, NSF/Box 338.
35. Rusk to Kennedy and "Background to Plan of Action for Indonesia," 2 October 962, and NSC Report: "Indonesia and Security, 1961–1963," January 1963, JFK Library, NSF and POF/Boxes 338 and 119.
36. Ibid. Michael V. Forrestal, Senior Staff, NSC, to the President, 15 October 1963, JFK Library, POF/Box 119.
37. Rusk to Kennedy, 2 October 1962, JFK Library, NSF/Box 338.
38. Office of the Secretary of State: Comments on Background to Plan of Action for Indonesia, 2 October 1962, ibid.
39. Ibid.

40. "Recommendations for Immediate Implementation – Civic Action Survey Team," Indonesia Report, State Department, October 2 1962, ibid.
41. Kennedy to Sukarno, 6 March 1963, ibid,; Pierre Salinger, *With Kennedy* (New York, 1966), p. 364.
42. Kennedy to Sukarno and Presidential Statement to Peace Corps Volunteers – Indonesia, July 1963, JFK Library, NSF/Box 338.
43. Sukarno to Kennedy, 18 August 1962, JFK Library, POF/Box 119.
44. Memorandum of Cabinet Discussion on Malaysian–Indonesian dispute, 19 November 1963, and Kennedy to Sukarno, 13 September, 1963, JFK Library, NSF/Box 338.
45. Kennedy to Sukarno, 14 May 1962, CIA Field Report – Djakarta and Jones to Kennedy, 1 October 1963, ibid.
46. National Security Council Memorandum: Indonesian Oil Negotiations, to Kennedy, 5 June 1963, ibid.
47. Memorandum of Conversation (The President, Jones, Hilsman, and Forrestal): "Visits: The President to Indonesia; General Nasution to Washington," Parts 1 and 2, 19 November 1963, ibid.
48. Ibid. (all of preceding note). Kennedy to Sukarno, 6 March 1963, ibid.
49. CIA Field Report – Djakarta, 1 October 1963, ibid.

5 "Holding the Beachhead" in the Philippines and Japan

1. State Department memorandum and report, "Country Date – Philippines (Background paper), Vice President's Visit to the Philippines, 8–16 May 1961," JFK Library, NSF/Box 242. Little has been written on Philippines nationalism in the early 1960s; however, one example of the phenomenon was the 1961 decision to take up the claim of the heirs of the Sultanate of Sulu to possession of the British colony of North Borneo. This regional claim, and the nationalist stirrings associated with it, is examined in: Lela G. Noble, *Philippine Policy Towards Sabah* (Tucson, 1977), Ralph Bernard Smith, *An International History of the Vietnam War: The Kennedy Strategy* (New York, 1985), pp. 136–7.
2. Richard Sneider, Officer in Charge, Japanese Affairs – State Department, to McGeorge Bundy, 23 June 1961, JFK Library, White House Central Files/Box 62.
3. George E. Taylor, *The Philippines and the United States: Problems of Partnership* (New York, 1964). This work examines the nature of US interests in the Philippines, suggesting ways to thwart Philippine nationalist sentiment. Other works condemn US "intrigue" in the Philippines, noting that Manila's problems with democracy are rooted in "American politics." The following work predicts the collapse of Philippine democracy by 1969. Robert Aura Smith, *Philippine Freedom, 1946–1958* (New York, 1958). Some Filipino writers, on the other hand, saw new challenges to America as positive, democracy-building developments. Remigio E. Agapalo, *The Political Process and the Nationalization of the Retail Trade in the Philippines* (Quezon City, 1962). Other Filipino writers concluded that the early 1960s illustrated America's

ignorance of Philippine affairs. They hoped to educate Americans on the basics of Philippine politics. Onofre D. Corpuz, *The Philippines* (Englewood Cliffs, 1965).

4. "Background paper: Vice President's Visit to the Philippines, May 8–16 1961," JFK Library, NSF/Box 242. The Philippines, and the problems it posed to the new Kennedy administration, has been examined in the framework of "difficult nations" facing "American power." Edwin O. Reischauer, *Beyond Vietnam: The United States and Asia* (New York, 1967) and John M. Maki, *Conflict and Tension in the Far East* (Seattle, 1961).

5. "Observations on Proposal for a New Pacific Community and Review of April Cabinet Session," 2 November 1961, JFK Library, NSF/Box 345.

6. "Background paper: Vice President's Visit to the Philippines, 8–16 May 1961," JFK Library, NSF/Box 242. The problem of development in the Philippines was the focus of two works by a leading Philippine nationalist, Carlos Romulo. See his: *Crusade in Asia* (New York, 1955) and Carlos Romulo and Marvin Gray, *The Magsaysay Story* (New York, 1956).

7. Ibid. (all of previous note). Rusk to Kennedy, May 8 1961, JFK Library, NSF/Box 345.

8. Ibid. Much has been written about the "Huk" rebellion, but one of the better accounts remains Alvin H. Scaff, *The Philippine Answer to Communism* (Stanford, 1955).

9. "Vice President's Visit to the Philippines – Foreign Affairs discussion, 8–16 May 1961," JFK Library, NSF/Box 345.

10. Ibid.

11. Ibid.

12. Ibid.

13. "Vice President's Visit to the Philippines – Sugar Quota discussions, 8–16 May 1961," JFK Library, NSF/Box 345.

14. Geoffrey B. Hainsworth, "Economic Growth and Poverty in Southeast Asia: Malaysia, Indonesia, and the Philippines," *Pacific Affairs*, Vol. 52 (Spring, 1979), pp. 5–41; A.V.H. Hartendorp, *History of Industry and Trade of the Philippines* (Manila, 1958), pp. 54, 730; Leslie E. Bauzon, *Philippine Agrarian Reform, 1880–1965* (Singapore, 1975).

15. "Vice President's Visit to the Philippines – Sugar Quota discussions, 8–16 May," JFK Library, NSF/Box 345.

16. Ibid.

17. Ibid., and "Report on the Vice President's Visit to the Philippines, 8–16 May 1961, JFK Library, NSF/Box 345.

18. "Vice President's Visit to the Philippines – Civil Air negotiations, 8–16 May, 1961," ibid. The Civil Aeronautics Board refused to grant special deals to an airline (PAL) that it considered incompetent. Memorandum on Civil Aeronautics Board Decision, Bureau of the Budget to Kennedy, 20 January 1962 January 1962, JFK Library, White House Central Files/ Box 32.

19. "Report on the Vice President's Visit to the Philippines, 8–16 May 1961", JFK Library, NSF/Box 345.

128 *Notes and References*

20. An even stronger view of America's longstanding connections with the Philippines is offered by Philippine politics specialist and communist activist, William Pomeroy. Pomeroy insists that the 1946 independence mandate actually bolstered American economic interests via special agreements, such as the sugar quota and miliatary base accords, *American Neo-Colonialism: Its Emergence in the Philippines and Asia* (New York, 1970).

21. "Vice President's Visit to the Philippines – War Damage legislation, 8–16 May 1961," JFK Library, NSF/Box 345; Gustav Ranis (ed.), *Sharing in Development: A Programme of Employment, Equity, and Growth for the Philippines* (Geneva, 1974), p. 10, and Ramon H. Myers, "The Roots of the Philippines Economic Troubles," *Asian Studies Center Backgrounder*, No. 14 (Washington, D.C., 1984).

22. "Vice President's Visit to the Philippines – War Damage Legislation, 8–16 May 1961," JFK Library, NSF/Box 345.

23. Ibid.

24. Ibid. Memorandum on H.R. 11721 (Zablocki War Damage Bill) and Kennedy to Congress, 30 August 1962, JFK Library, POF/Box 39.

25. "Vice President's Visit to the Philippines – Military Bases negotiations, 8–16 May 1961," JFK Library, NSF/Box 345.

26. A. James Gregor, *Crisis in the Philippines: A Threat to U.S. Interests* (Washington, D.C., 1984), pp. 16–17.

27. "Vice President's Visit to the Philippines – Military Bases negotiations, 8–16 May 1961," JFK Library, NSF/Box 345.

28. Ronnie Dugger, *The Politician: The Life and Times of Lyndon Johnson – The Drive for Power, from the Frontier to Master of the Senate* (New York, 1982), pp. 382–99.

29. Eric Goldman, Special Consultant to Johnson, recalled an assistant secretary of state complaining that Johnson would be a poor representative of America in Asia. "Like some wines," he heard this official state, "Lyndon does not travel well." Johnson left the Philippines for discussions with Thai, Vietnamese, and Indian politicians, because, Kennedy said, his Vice President needed something to do. It also heightened the importance of Asia in American foreign affairs. Johnson, Goldman remembered, thought Asian affairs were easier to understand than European politics. "Asia lit all kinds of candles in his mind. This was especially true because rural, impoverished Asia, in contrast to industrialized, prospering Europe, evoked memories of his native central Texas." Eric F. Goldman, *The Tragedy of Lyndon Johnson* (New York, 1969), pp. 386–7.

30. "Vice President's Visit to the Philippines – U.S. Military Assistance Program (MAP) discussions, 8–16 May 1961," JFK Library, NSF/Box 345.

31. Ibid.

32. Ibid. No President of the 1960s wanted to be considered "soft on communism" in an era of communist growth. Kennedy's political fears over such considerations were inherited by his successors, and those fears were often manifested in the use of ground troops. This conclusion is a

major thesis point of George McT. Kahin, *Intervention: How America Became Involved in Vietnam* (New York, 1986).

33. State Department Background Paper: MAP–1961 (Philippines), and "Vice President's Visit to the Philippines – U.S. Military Assistance Program (MAP) discussions, 8–16 May 1961," JFK Library, NSF/Box 345.

34. "Problems in MAP Management (Philippines)," May 8–16 1961, and Frederick G. Dutton to Kennedy, 8 September 1961, JFK Library, NSF/Box 345 and White House Central Files/Box 67.

35. Garcia to Kennedy, 24 May 1961, JFK Library, POF/Box 123a.

36. Macapagal to Kennedy, 14 May 1962, The remarks of the newly appointed Ambassador to the United States from the Philippines, Amelito R. Mutuc, upon the occasion of the presentation of his Letter of Credence, November 1962, Macapagal to Kennedy, 31 August 1962, JFK Library, POF/Box 123a, White House Central Files/Box 67.

37. Macapagal to Kennedy, 17 June 1963, JFK Library, POF/Box 123a.

38. Ibid. Rusk to Kennedy and Kennedy to Rusk, August 12, and 14, 1963, JFK Library, White House Central Files/Box 67.

39. Steve Frantzich, "Party Switching in the Philippine Context," *Philippine Studies*, Vol. 16 (October 1968), pp. 750–768.

40. Ferdinand E. Marcos, *The Democratic Revolution in the Philippines* (Englewood Cliffs, 1979), p. 26.

41. Briefing Material: Visit of Prime Minister Ikeda, State Department to Kennedy, 23 June 1961, JFK Library, POF/Box 120.

42. Shigeru Yoshida, *The Yoshida Memoirs: The Story of Japan in Crisis* (Boston, 1962), pp. 254–75; Bernard C. Cohen, *The Political Process and Foreign Policy: The Making of the Japanese Peace Settlement* (Princeton, 1957), p. 20; State Department, *Department of State Bulletin*, Vol. 42 (8 February 1960), pp. 180, 184–201.

43. Dan Kurzman, *Kishi and Japan: The Search for the Sun* (New York, 1960), p. 326.

44. Herbert Passin (ed.), *The United States and Japan* (Englewood Cliffs, 1966), pp. 29–56. Like many foreign observers, the Japanese people would be entertained by Kennedy's wit and charm; however, they also worried that youth brought inexperience and rash action to American foreign policy-making. James C. Thomson, Jr, *et al.*, *Sentimental Imperialists: The American Experience in East Asia* (New York, 1985), p. 303.

45. Ralph E. Lapp, *The Voyage of the Lucky Dragon* (New York, 1958).

46. Sherman Adams, *Firsthand Report: The Story of the Eisenhower Administration* (New York, 1961), pp. 409–12.

47. Japan's debate over the Treaty, in all its anger and emotion, is analyzed in George W. Packard III, *Protest in Tokyo: The Security Treaty Crisis of 1960* (Princeton, 1966). See also Herbert Kahn, *The Emerging Japanese Superstate* (Englewood Cliffs, 1970), ch. 2; Graham T. Allison, "American Foreign Policy and Japan," Henry Rosovsky (ed.), *Discord in the Pacific* (Washington, D.C., 1972).

48. Briefing Material: Visit of Prime Minister Ikeda, State Department to Kennedy, June 23 1961, JFK Library, POF/Box 120.

49. Bernard C. Cohen, *The Press and Foreign Policy* (Princeton, 1965), p.

251; Priscilla Clapp, "U.S. Domestic Politics and Relations with Japan," Priscilla Clapp and Morton Halperin (eds.), *United States–Japanese Relations: The 1970s* (Cambridge, Mass., 1974), pp. 35–57.

50. R.K. Jain, *China and Japan, 1949–76* (Atlantic Highlands, NJ, 1977), pp. 67–68; US and USSR trade relations during the Ikeda years is a major focus of Chitoshi Yanaga, *Big Business in Japanese Politics* (New Haven, 1968).

51. "Observations on Proposal for a New Pacific Community and Review of April Cabinet Session," 2 November 1961, JFK Library, NSF/Box 345.

52. Lawrence F. O'Brien, Special Assistant to the President, to Rep. John Baldwin, 8 March 1961, JFK Library, White House Central Files/Box 62.

53. Lawrence F. O'Brien to Rep. Leo W. O'Brien and O'Brien Bill, 4 May 1961, .JFK Library, White House Central Files/Box 62.

54. Ibid.

55. Minutes of Kennedy–Ikeda discussion, 20–21 June 1961, "Joint Communiqué issued by the President and Prime Minister Hayato Ikeda of Japan," 22 June 1961, and Kennedy to Henry Luce, *Time/Life*, 10 July 1961, JFK Library, POF/Box 120 and White House Central Files/Box 62.

56. Ibid. (all of preceding note). For the "special considerations" of the Ryukyus issue, see the following chapter.

57. Memorandum and Report for Frederick P. Dutton, White House: The United States–Japanese Committee, 12 October 1961, JFK Library, White House Central Files/Box 62.

58. Ibid.

59. Ibid. Reischauer worried that the American government exaggerated anti-American sentiment in Japan and its significance in Japanese politics. He welcomed Kennedy's "cooperative spirit," suggesting that Japan deserved as much attention from Washington as Southeast Asia. The New Pacific Community approach promised to create that attentive policy. Edwin O. Reischauer, "An Overview," in Clapp and Halperin, *United States–Japanese Relations: The 1970s*, pp. 1–18; "The Broken Dialogue with Japan," *Foreign Affairs*, Vol. 39 (October 1960), pp. 11–16.

60. McGovern to Sen. Wayne Morse, 13 October 1961, JFK Library, White House Central Files/Box 62.

61. Hauge to the White House and report on trade delegation meetings, October 1961–February 1962, 27 February 1962, JFK Library, White House Central Files/Box 62.

62. "Proclamation Giving Effect to Trade Agreement Negotiations with Japan," 1 February 1963, JFK Library, POF/Box 120.

63. Reischauer's interest in a peaceful world did not mean that he opposed America's security interests in the region. The balance of power in the Pacific, he believed, required Japan to become America's "reliable partner." Donald C. Hellmann, *Japan and East Asia: The New International Order* (New York, 1972), pp. 117, 131. Ikeda to Kennedy, 2 March 1962, JFK Library, POF/Box 120.

64. Ibid.
65. Memorandum of Conversation on US–Japanese relations (State Department Policy Planning Staff and guests), 19 June 1962, JFK Library, POF/Box 120.
66. Ibid.
67. Ibid.
68. Ibid.
69. Memorandum for Kenneth O'Donnell, Special Assistant to the President: Sato and Industrial Tour, 19 September 1962, and Sato to Kennedy, October 1962, JFK Library, White House Central Files/Box 62 and POF/Box 120.
70. Ikeda to Kennedy, 25 October 1962, JFK Library, POF/Box 120. Japanese opinion on nuclear development remained in conflict with the desire to modernize the nation. Balancing "progress" with anti-nuclear policies complicated the Japanese view of war and peace. This problem, and particularly the role of the press within it, is explored in John K. Emmerson, *Arms, Yen, and Power: The Japanese Dilemma* (New York, 1971).
71. Roenigk to McNamara: Department of Defense Intelligence Information Report: Japan, 8 July 1963, JFK Library, POF/Box 120.
72. Rusk to Reischauer and Kennedy to Ikeda, 25 July 1963, JFK Library, POF/Box 120.
73. Ikeda to Kennedy, 31 July 1963, JFK Library, POF/Box 120.
74. Ibid.
75. Kennedy to the United States–Japan Conference on Cultural and Educational Interchange, 15 October 1963, JFK Library, White House Central Files/Box 62.

6   Assumption and "Special Considerations:" The Ryukus

1. Quoted in Passin, *The United States and Japan*, p. 73.
2. United States Civil Administration of the Ryukyu Islands (USCAR), *Ryukyu Islands, 1950–1956* (Okinawa, 1956), introduction; USCAR, *Joint Economic Plan for the Ryukyu Islands, 1961–1965* (Okinawa, 1965), introduction; Briefing Material to Prime Minister Ikeda's visit, State Department to Kennedy, 23 June 1961, JFK Library, POF/Box 120. Although the comparisons between the long American role at Guam and the relatively recent occupation of Okinawa were not always clear, they were difficult to avoid. Both were prizes of war, strategically valuable, and rife with political problems.
3. Military studies of the battle for Okinawa abound. The following work stands out from the others due to its consideration of the psychological impact of the battle on Japanese society. William P. Simpson, *Island X – Okinawa* (W. Hanover, Mass., 1981).
4. Career diplomat and containment thesis author, George Kennan, helped Truman restructure the American role in the Ryukyus. See his "Japan's Security and American Policy," *Foreign Affairs*, Vol. 43 (October 1964), pp. 14–28.

5. Treating Okinawa as if it was a piece of military hardware was characteristic of the Eisenhower approach. See the Defense Department's position paper on the Ryukyus in US Congress, Committee on Appropriations, *Mutual Security Appropriations for 1961 and Related Agencies, Hearings Before the Subcommittee of the Committee on Appropriations, House of Representatives*, 86th Cong., 2nd Sess. (Washington, 1960).

6. The government structure of the American occupation, in its entire complexity, is well described in USCAR, *Civil Affairs Statistics of the Ryukyu Islands, 1950–1972* (Okinawa, 1972).

7. Although highly emotional and filled with visions of a coming new era of American–Ryukyuan–Japanese relations, Mikio Higa's account of local politics from the Truman era to Johnson remains vital to any serious student of the Ryukyus debate. Mikio Higa, *Politics and Parties in Postwar Okinawa* (Vancouver, 1963).

8. US Office of Armed Forces Information and Education, *A Pocket Guide to Okinawa* (Washington, D.C., 1961). A fading way of life in the face of American encroachment is the major thesis point of Douglas G. Haring, *Okinawan Customs: Yesterday and Today* (Rutland, Vt., 1969); USCAR, *Economic Plan for the Ryukyu Islands, 1951* (Okinawa, 1951), and *Joint Economic Plan for the Ryukyu Islands, 1961–1965*.

9. Ibid. (all of preceding note).

10. Observations on Proposal for a New Pacific Community and Review of April Cabinet Session, 2 November 1961, JFK Library, NSF/Box 345.

11. Ibid. Kennedy's decision is reviewed in Col. W. A. Kelley, Assistant Civil Administrator, USCAR, to Lawrence O'Brien, 12 May 1961, JFK Library, White House Central Files/Box 691.

12. Ibid.

13. Kennedy's negative view of the Kelley thesis, and his desire for a working policy, was clear in his 11 August 1961 task force request to the National Security Council, JFK Library, POF/Box 123b.

14. The Ryukyus issue was a significant one in Japanese politics, and Japanese politicians and foreign policy-makers were amazed that Washington did not appreciate its delicate nature. This point is stressed in Akio Watanabe, *The Okinawa Problem: A Chapter in Japan–U.S. Relations* (Carlton, Australia, 1970). Nevertheless, the issue should also be viewed in the context of the intense Liberal *v.* Socialist struggle in Japan during the early 1960s. See J. A. A. Stockwin, *The Japanese Socialist Party and Neutralism* (Carlton, Australia, 1968), and Nathaniel P. Thayer, *How the Conservatives Rule Japan* (Princeton, 1969).

15. Briefing Material to Prime Minister Ikeda's visit, State Department to Kennedy, 23 June 1961, JFK Library, POF/Box 120.

16. Kennedy admits his preference for Reischauer's reports in his lengthy task force instructions to the National Security Council, 11 August 1961, JFK Library, POF/Box 123b.

17. Report and Recommendations of the Task Force Ryukyus, December 1961, JFK Library, POF/Box 123b.

18. Visit of Prime Minister Ikeda – Ryukyus, 23 June 1961, JFK Library, POF/Box 120.

19. Memorandum on All Nippon Airways Company, Ltd, Bureau of the

Budget, to Kennedy, June 28, 1961, JFK Library, White House Central Files/Box 31.

20. Report and Recommendations of the Task Force Ryukyus, December 1961, JFK Library, POF/Box 123b.

21. Seisaku Ota, Chief Executive, Government of the Ryukyu Islands, to Kennedy, 26 March 1962, JFK Library, White House Central Files/Box 572.

22. Carl Kaysen, Deputy Special Assistant to the President for National Security Affairs, to GRI and Ryukyuans-abroad petitioners, 6 June 1962, JFK Library, White House Central Files/Box 825.

23. Ikeda's and the GRI's concern, as well as Kennedy's caution, are considered in Ministry of Foreign Affairs – Tokyo, Public Information Bureau, *Okinawa: Some Basic Facts* (Tokyo, 1969). A vigorous defense of Kennedy's security priorities is offered in James H. McBride and the Directorate of Documentary Research, Air University Institute for Professional Development, Maxwell Air Force Base, *Okinawa: Pawn in the Pacific* (Maxwell Air Force Base, 1972). A cynical treatment of all positions in the Ryukyus debate is the approach offered by William G. Ross, *Why to Okinawa?* (North Quincy, Mass., 1971).

24. Ota to Kennedy, 26 March 1962, JFK Library, White House Central Files/Box 572.

25. P. Arakaki and Jon J. Chinen to Kennedy, 9 May 1962, JFK Library, White House Central Files/Box 26.

26. Kennedy's practical accomplishments and impact on the issue were considered in USCAR, Office of the High Commissioner, *Final Report, May 14, 1972* (Okinawa, 1972), and US Congress, House Committee on Foreign Affairs, Subcommittee on the Far East and the Pacific, *Claims of Certain Inhabitants of the Ryukyu Islands*, Hearing, 89th Cong., 1st Sess., 28 July 1965 (Washington, D.C., 1965).

27. Department of State, *Reversion to Japan of the Ryukyu Islands. Agreement Between the United States of America and Japan signed at Washington and Tokyo, June 17, 1971 with Related Arrangements* (Washington, 1972).

Conclusions

1. Quoted in Sorensen, *The Kennedy Legacy*, p. 254.
2. Fairlie, *Kennedy Promise*, p. 288.

Bibliography

PRIMARY

Unpublished material
The Library of the President John F. Kennedy, Boston, Massachusetts
    Collections:

    Senate Files
    Biographical Files
    President's Official Files (POF)
    National Security Files (NSF)
    Guam and Pacific Files
    White House Central Files
    Personal Papers

National Archives, Washington, D.C.
Collection:

    Record Group 273, Records of the National Security Council 1961–1963

The Micronesian Area Research Center, University of Guam Collections:

    Confidential Files of the Pacific Collection, *Micronesian Reporter*

Personal Correspondence

    "Events leading to the formation of the Office of Micronesian Status Negotiations," Report of the Subcommittee on Asian/Pacific Affairs, House of Representatives, submitted to author, July 1985.

ANALYTICAL, NARRATIVE AND PUBLISHED PRIMARY WORKS

Books
ADAMS, CINDY, *Sukarno* (Indianapolis: Bobbs-Merrill, 1965).
ADAMS, SHERMAN. *Firsthand Report: The Story of the Eisenhower Administration* (New York: Harper, 1961).
AGAPALO, REMIGIO E. *The Political Process and the Nationalization of the Retail Trade in the Philippines* (Quezon City: University of the Philippines Press, 1962).
ALLISON, GRAHAM T. "American Foreign Policy and Japan," in Henry

Rosovsky (ed.), *Discord in the Pacific* (Washington, D.C.: Columbia Books, 1972).

BAUZON, LESLIE E. *Philippine Agrarian Reform, 1880–1965* (Singapore: Institute of Southeast Asian Studies, 1975).

BUEHRIG, EDWARD H. (ed.) *Wilson's Foreign Policy in Perspective* (Bloomington, Ind.: University of Indiana Press, 1957).

BURNER, DAVID and THOMAS R. WEST. *The Torch is Passed: The Kennedy Brothers and American Liberalism* (New York: Atheneum, 1984).

BURNS, JAMES MACGREGOR. *Edward Kennedy and the Camelot Legacy* (New York: Norton, 1976).

CLAPP, PRISCILLA and MORTON HALPERIN (eds), *United States-Japanese Relations: The 1970s* (Cambridge, Mass: Harvard University Press, 1974).

COHEN, BERNARD C. *The Political Process and Foreign Policy: The Making of the Japanese Peace Settlement* (Princeton: Princeton University Press, 1957).

COHEN, BERNARD C. *The Press and Foreign Policy* (Princeton: Princeton University Press, 1965).

CORPUZ, ONOFRE E. *The Philippines* (Englewood Cliffs: Prentice-Hall, 1965).

DUGGER, RONNIE. *The Politician: The Life and Times of Lyndon Johnson – The Drive for Power from the Frontier to Master of the Senate* (New York: Norton, 1982).

EMMERSON, JOHN K. *Arms, Yen, and Power: The Japanese Dilemma* (New York: Dunellen, 1971).

ENTHOVEN, ALAIN C. and K. WAYNE SMITH. *How Much Is Enough? Shaping the Defense Program, 1961–1969* (New York: Harper, 1971).

FAIRLIE, HENRY. *The Kennedy Promise: The Politics of Expectation* (New York: Doubleday, 1973).

FITZSIMONS, LOUISE. *The Kennedy Doctrine* (New York: Random House, 1972).

GELBER, HARRY G. *Australia, Britain and the EEC, 1961–1963* (Melbourne: Oxford University Press, 1966).

GOLDMAN, ERIC F. *The Tragedy of Lyndon Johnson* (New York: Knopf, 1969).

GRAVEL, THE SENATOR EDITION. *The Pentagon Papers: The Defense Department History of the United States Decisionmaking on Vietnam*, 4 vols (Boston: Beacon Press, 1971).

GREGOR, A. JAMES. *Crisis in the Philippines: A Threat to U.S. Interests* (Washington, D.C.: Ethics and Public Policy Center, 1984).

HALBERSTAM, DAVID. *The Best and the Brightest* (New York: Random House, 1972).

HARING, DOUGLAS G. *Okinawan Customs: Yesterday and Today* (Rutland, Vt.: Charles E. Tuttle, 1969).

HARTENDORP, A. V. H. *History of Industry and Trade of the Philippines* (Manila: American Chamber of Commerce, 1958).

HELLMAN, DONALD C. *Japan and East Asia: The New International Order* (New York: Praeger, 1972).

HIGA, MIKIO. *Politics and Parties in Postwar Okinawa* (Vancouver: Publications Center of the University of British Columbia, 1963).

HILSMAN, ROGER. *To Move a Nation: The Politics of Foreign Policy in the Administration of John F. Kennedy* (New York: Doubleday, 1967).

HUGHES, DANIEL T. and SHERWOOD G. LINGENFELTER. *Political Development in Micronesia* (Columbus: Ohio State University Press, 1974).

JAIN, RAJENDRA K. *China and Japan, 1949–76* (Atlantic Highlands, NJ: Humanities Press, 1977).

JONES, HOWARD P. *Indonesia: The Possible Dream* (New York: Harcourt Brace Jovanovich, 1971).

KAHIN, GEORGE McT. *Intervention: How America Became Involved in Vietnam* (New York: Knopf, 1986).

KAHN, E. J., Jr. *A Reporter in Micronesia* (New York: Norton, 1966).

KAHN, HERBERT. *The Emerging Japanese Superstate* (Englewood Cliffs: Prentice-Hall, 1970).

KENNEDY, EDWARD M. (ed.) *The Fruitful Bough: A Tribute to Joseph P. Kennedy* (Boston: Private Publication, 1966).

KENNEDY, JOHN F. *Profiles in Courage* (New York: Harper, 1956).

KENNEDY, JOHN F. *Public Papers of the President, 1961–1963* (Washington, D.C.: GPO, 1962–1964).

KERN, MONTAGUE, PATRICIA LEVERING and RALPH LEVERING. *The Kennedy Crises: The Press, the Presidency, and Foreign Policy* (Chapel Hill: University of North Carolina Press, 1983).

KOLKO, GABRIEL. *Anatomy of War: Vietnam, the United States, and the Modern Historical Experience* (New York: Pantheon, 1985).

KOSUT, HAL (ed.) *Indonesia: The Sukarno Years* (New York: Facts on File, 1970).

KURZMAN, DAN. *Kishi and Japan: The Search for the Sun* (New York: I. Obolensky, 1960).

LAPP, RALPH E. *The Voyage of the Lucky Dragon* (New York: Harper, 1958).

LEDERER, WILLIAM J., and EUGENE BURDICK. *The Ugly American* (New York: Norton, 1960).

LEUCTENBURG, WILLIAM. *In the Shadow of FDR: From Harry Truman to Ronald Reagan* (Ithaca: Cornell University Press, 1983).

LOWI, THEODORE, J. *The Personal President: Power Invested, Promise Unfulfilled* (Ithaca: Cornell University Press, 1985).

McBRIDE, JAMES H. and the DIRECTORATE OF DOCUMENTARY RESEARCH, AIR UNIVERSITY INSTITUTE FOR PROFESSIONAL DEVELOPMENT, MAXWELL AIR FORCE BASE. *Okinawa: Pawn in the Pacific* (Maxwell Air Force Base: Air University for Professional Development, 1972).

MAGA, TIMOTHY P. "The Promise Fulfilled: John F. Kennedy and the New Frontier in Guam and the Trust Territory of the Pacific Islands, 1961–1963," in Alexj Ugrinsky (ed.), *JFK* (Westport, Conn.: Greenwood, 1985).

MAHONEY, RICHARD D. *JFK: Ordeal in Africa* (New York: Oxford University Press, 1983).

MAKI, JOHN M. *Conflict and Tension in the Far East* (Seattle: University of Washington Press, 1961).

MARCOS, FERDINAND E. *The Democratic Revolution in the Philippines* (Englewood Cliffs: Prentice-Hall, 1979).

MINISTRY OF FOREIGN AFFAIRS – TOKYO, PUBLIC INFORMATION BUREAU. *Okinawa: Some Basic Facts* (Tokyo: Ministry of Foreign Affairs, 1969).

NASUTION, GEN. ABDUL H. *The Indonesian National Army* (Djakarta: Jajasan Pustaka Militer, 1956).

NEVIN, DAVID. *The American Touch in Micronesia* (New York: Norton, 1977).

NOBLE, LELA G. *Philippine Policy Towards Sabah* (Tucson: University of Arizona Press, 1977).

PACKARD, GEORGE W. III. *Protest in Tokyo: The Security Treaty Crisis of 1960* (Princeton: Princeton University Press, 1966).

PAPER, LEWIS. *The Promise and the Performance: The Leadership of John F. Kennedy* (New York: Crown, 1975).

PARMET, HERBERT. *Jack: The Struggles of John F. Kennedy* (New York: Dial Press, 1980).

PASSIN, HERBERT (ed). *The United States and Japan* (Englewood Cliffs: Prentice-Hall, 1966).

POMEROY, EARL S. *Pacific Outpost: American Strategy in Guam and Micronesia* (Stanford: Stanford University Press, 1951).

POMEROY, WILLIAM. *American Neo-Colonialism: Its Emergence in the Philippines and Asia* (New York: International Publishers, 1970).

RANIS, GUSTAV (ed.) *Sharing in Development: A Programme of Employment, Equity, and Growth for the Philippines* (Geneva: International Labor Organization, 1974).

REESE, TREVOR. *Australia, New Zealand, and the United States, 1941–1968* (London: Oxford University Press, 1969).

REISCHAUER, EDWIN O. *Beyond Vietnam: The United States and Asia* (New York: Knopf, 1967).

ROMULO, CARLOS. *Crusade in Asia* (New York: J. Day, 1955).

ROMULO, CARLOS and MARVIN GRAY. *The Magsaysay Story*. (New York: J. Day, 1956).

ROSS, WILLIAM G. *Why to Okinawa?* (North Quincy, Mass.: Christopher Publishing House, 1971).

RUST, WILLIAM. *Kennedy in Vietnam* (New York: Charles Scribner's Sons, 1985).

SALINGER, PIERRE. *With Kennedy* (New York: Doubleday, 1966).

SCAFF, ALVIN H. *The Philippines Answer to Communism* (Stanford: Stanford University Press, 1955).

SCHLESINGER, ARTHUR, M., Jr. *A Thousand Days: John F. Kennedy in the White House* (Boston: Houghton Mufflin, 1965).

SCHLESINGER, ARTHUR M., Jr. *Robert Kennedy and His Times* (New York: Houghton Mifflin, 1978).

SIMON, SHELDON W. *Broken Triangle: Peking, Djakarta, and the PKI* (Baltimore: Johns Hopkins Press, 1969).

SIMPSON, WILLIAM P. *Island X-Okinawa* (W. Hanover, Mass.: Christopher Publishing House, 1981).

SMITH, RALPH BERNARD. *An International History of the Vietnam War: The Kennedy Strategy* (New York: St. Martin's Press, 1985).

SMITH, ROBERT AURA. *Philippine Freedom, 1946–1958* (New York: Columbia University Press, 1958).

SORENSEN, THEODORE C. *Decision-Making in the White House* (New York: Columbia University Press, 1964).

SORENSEN, THEODORE C. *The Kennedy Legacy* (New York: Macmillan, 1969).

STOCKWIN, J. A. A. *The Japanese Socialist Party and Neutralism* (Carlton, Australia: Melbourne University Press, 1968).

TAYLOR, GEORGE E. *The Philippines and the United States: Problems of Partnership* (New York: Praeger, 1964).

THAYER, NATHANIEL. *How the Conservatives Rule Japan* (Princeton: Princeton University Press, 1969).

THOMSON, JAMES C. Jr, *et al. Sentimental Imperialists: The American Experience in East Asia* (New York: Harper Torchbooks, 1985).

UNITED NATIONS GENERAL ASSEMBLY, *Report on Micronesia, 1964* (New York: United Nations, 1964).

UNITED STATES CIVIL ADMINISTRATION OF THE RYUKYU ISLANDS (USCAR). *Civil Affairs Statistics of the Ryukyu Islands 1950–1972* (Okinawa: USCAR, 1972).

USCAR. *Economic Plan for the Ryukyu Islands, 1951* (Okinawa, USCAR, 1951).

USCAR. *Joint Economic Plan for the Ryukyu Islands, 1961–1965* (Okinawa: USCAR, 1965).

USCAR, Office of the High Commissioner. *Final Report, May 14, 1972* (Okinawa: USCAR, 1972).

USCAR. *Ryukyu Islands, 1950–1956* (Okinawa: USCAR, 1956).

UNITED STATES CONGRESS, Committee on Appropriations. *Mutual Security Appropriations for 1961 and Related Agencies, Hearings Before the Subcommittee of the Committee on Appropriations, House of Representatives.* 86th Cong., 2nd Sess. (Washington, D.C.: GPO, 1960).

UNITED STATES CONGRESS, House of Representatives Committee on Foreign Affairs, Subcommittee on the Far East and the Pacific. *Claims of Certain Inhabitants of the Ryukyu Islands.* 89th Cong., 1st Sess. (Washington, D.C.: GPO, 1965).

UNITED STATES DEPARTMENT OF STATE. *Reversion to Japan of the Ryukyu Islands. Agreement Between the United States of America and Japan signed at Washington and Tokyo, June 17, 1971 with Related Arrangements* (Washington, D.C.: GPO, 1972).

UNITED STATES DEPARTMENT OF STATE. *The Sino-Soviet Economic Offensive Through June 30, 1962* (Washington, D.C.: Unclassified Research Memorandum RSB–145, 18 September 1962).

UNITED STATES OFFICE OF ARMED FORCES INFORMATION AND EDUCATION. *A Pocket Guide to Okinawa* (Washington, D.C.: GPO, 1961).

WALTON, RICHARD. *Cold War and Counterrevolution: The Foreign Policy of John F. Kennedy* (New York: Viking, 1972).
WATANABE, AKIO. *The Okinawa Problem: A Chapter in Japan-U.S. Relations* (Carlton, Australia: Melbourne University Press, 1970).
WEBB, JAMES H., Jr. *Micronesia and U.S. Pacific Strategy: A Blueprint for the 1980s* (New York: Praeger, 1974).
WILLS, GARRY. *The Kennedy Imprisonment: A Meditation on Power* (Boston: Little, Brown, 1982).
YANAGA, CHITOSHI. *Big Business in Japanese Politics* (New Haven: Yale University Press, 1968).
YOSHIDA, SHIGERU. *The Yoshida Memoirs: The Story of Japan in Crisis* (Boston: Houghton Mifflin, 1962).

Articles

ALBINSKI, H. S. "Australia and the Dutch New Guinea Dispute." *International Journal*, Autumn 1961, 358–62.
DENOON, DAVID. "Indonesia: Transition to Stability?" *Current History*, Vol 61, 1971, 332–38.
EMBASSY OF INDONESIA, WASHINGTON, D.C. *PIA News Bulletin*, Vols 1960–1963. Washington, D.C.: Indonesia Information Service, 1960–63.
FRANTZICH, STEVE. "Party Switching in the Philippine Context," *Philippine Studies*, Vol. 16, October 1968, 750–68.
HAINSWORTH, GEOFFREY B. "Economic Growth and Poverty in Southeast Asia: Malaysia, Indonesia, and the Philippines," *Pacific Affairs*, Vol. 52, Spring 1979, pp. 5–41.
KENNAN, GEORGE. "Japan's Security and American Policy," *Foreign Affairs*, Vol. 43, October 1964, pp. 14–28.
MAGA, TIMOTHY P. "The Citizenship Movement in Guam, 1946–1950," *Pacific Historical Review*, Vol. 53, February 1984, 59–77.
MALONE, MIKE. "The CIA in Micronesia," *Glimpses of Micronesia*, Vol. 23, 1983, pp. 28–30.
MYERS, RAMON H. "The Roots of the Philippines' Economic Troubles," *Asian Studies Center Backgrounder*, No. 14, Heritage Foundation, 1984.
RAWSON, D. W. "Foreign Policy and Australian Parties," *World Review*, July 1962, pp. 16–23.
REISCHAUER, EDWIN O. "The Broken Dialogue with Japan," *Foreign Affairs*, Vol. 39, October 1960, pp. 11–16.
STAFF REPORT. "Indonesia's Armoury," *Far Eastern Economic Review* (Hong Kong). 1 November, 1962, pp. 283–4.
UNITED STATES DEPARTMENT OF STATE. *Department of State Bulletin*, Vol. 42, 8 February 1960, pp. 180–201.
WILCYNSKI, J. "Australia's Trade With China," *India Quarterly*, April-June 1965, pp. 154–67.
WOODWARD, BOB. "CIA Bugging Micronesia Negotiations," *The Washington Post*, 12 December 1976.

Dissertation

NURSE, RONALD. "America Must Not Sleep: The Development of John F. Kennedy's Foreign Policy Attitudes, 1947–1960." Unpublished Ph.D. dissertation, Michigan State University, 1971.

Index

141